AEI SPECIAL ANALYSES
*Timely examinations of issues being debated
in the formulation of public policy*

Achieving Financial Solvency in Social Security

Mickey D. Levy

AMERICAN ENTERPRISE INSTITUTE
FOR PUBLIC POLICY RESEARCH
Washington and London

This study was prepared for an AEI Conference on Controlling the Cost of Social Security, June 25–26, 1981. Colin Campbell and Thomas Johnson, co-chairmen of the conference, and the conference discussants of the paper, Robert Myers, Robert Reischauer, and J. J. Van Gorkom, provided helpful comments. In addition, I would like to thank Arthur Broida and Debbie Thullen of AEI. Important program information and data were provided by Ken Sander of the Social Security Administration and Steve Chaikind and Bob Staiger of the Congressional Budget Office.

Distributed to the Trade by National Book Network, 15200 NBN Way, Blue Ridge Summit, PA 17214. To order call toll free 1-800-462-6420 or 1-717-794-3800. For all other inquiries please contact the AEI Press, 1150 Seventeenth Street, N.W., Washington, D.C. 20036 or call 1-800-862-5801.

ISBN 0-8447-1094-6

Library of Congress Catalog Card No. 81-69347
Special Analysis No. 81-6

CONTENTS

1

INTRODUCTION

The Social Security Amendments of 1972 capped nearly four decades of continuous expansion and benefit increases by boosting benefits a generous 20 percent and indexing benefits to inflation beginning in 1975. At the time, the social security trust fund balances were considered sufficient to absorb any temporary deficit caused by adverse conditions, while projections based on robust fertility rates and a stable and growing economy showed large long-run actuarial surpluses. Since 1973, social security financing has not been viewed through such rose-colored glasses. Annual reports of the trustees of the social security system began projecting long-run deficits based on lower long-run fertility rates and higher rates of inflation and unemployment than were assumed previously. An indexing flaw in the 1972 amendments was detected in 1974 which, until modified by the 1977 amendments, added substantially to projected long-run deficits of the program. Also in the mid-1970s, high rates of unemployment and inflation, coupled with declining growth rates of real wages, precipitated a rapid decline in trust fund balances. In 1977, Congress responded to the short-run financial crisis by increasing payroll taxes, but it largely ignored the long-run financing issue.

Declines in the growth of real wages have more than offset the higher payroll taxes in the 1977 amendments and once again are forcing Congress and the Reagan administration to come to the rescue of the social security system. Concurrently, Congress needs to grapple head-on with the projected seventy-five-year financing deficit resulting from assumed declines in birth and mortality rates and the trend toward early retirement. Congress naturally tends to postpone making unpopular decisions. This problem of political expedience versus economic reality has been accommodated by recent official reports on social security—for example, by the 1979 Advisory Council on Social Security and the National Commission on Social Security. Despite projecting long-run actuarial deficits, these reports in general have not thoroughly considered the issue of the affordability of future scheduled benefits and have implied that there is no immediate need to address the long-run issue. Quite the contrary, however, some potential modifications of the system, such as changing the benefit formula or the age of retirement, may take several years to implement on a fair basis, and they should be addressed without delay.

The next chapter of this study outlines the nature and causes of the financing problems, particularly those that have developed since the 1977 amendments. Chapter 3 reviews the short-run financing projections of the 1979 Advisory Council, the trustees' *1980 Annual Report,* the National Commission on Social Security (NCSS), and the trustees' *1981 Annual Report,* and compares the economic assumptions underlying them.[1] The fourth chapter considers ways to close the short-run gap between social security benefits and taxes. The final chapter deals with the long-run financing issue, emphasizing the apparent conflict between the goal of high benefits and affordability.

Four conclusions arise from this analysis:

- The social security financing issue has two sides—benefits and taxes—and, in light of dramatic long-run demographic shifts and uncertain financial forecasts, currently scheduled benefits should no longer be considered sacrosanct.
- Benefits can be trimmed selectively so that truly needy recipients are not affected.
- Accounting changes, such as interfund transfers, should not be relied on entirely to resolve the short-run financing problem.
- Solutions to the projected long-run deficit should be achieved by this Congress.

NOTE TO CHAPTER 1

[1] U.S. Department of Health, Education and Welfare, Advisory Council on Social Security, *Social Security Financing and Benefits,* December 1979; Board of Trustees, Federal Old-Age and Survivors Insurance, Disability Insurance, and Hospital Insurance Trust Funds, *1980 Annual Report,* 1980; National Commission on Social Security, *Social Security in America's Future,* March 1981; Board of Trustees, Federal Old-Age and Survivors Insurance, Disability Insurance, and Hospital Insurance Trust Funds, *1981 Annual Report,* 1981.

2

THE NATURE AND CAUSES OF THE FINANCIAL PROBLEM

The short-term financing problem facing social security's largest cash program, Old-Age and Survivors Insurance (OASI), is serious and will require corrective action by 1982 if scheduled benefits are to be fully financed by the OASI trust fund. The other two major social security trust funds, for Disability Insurance (DI) and Hospital Insurance (HI), are in better financial shape, largely as a consequence of the Social Security Amendments of 1977 (Public Law 95-216), which increased payroll taxes designated for the DI and HI trust funds, and the Disability Amendments of 1980 (Public Law 96-265), which tightened administrative procedures for the program. Both the DI and the HI trust fund contingency reserves are now projected to remain at adequate levels through the mid-1980s. According to several recent reports, however, the combined OASDHI trust funds are expected to be inadequate after 1984, so that even if the OASI trust fund is allowed to borrow from the other two funds, the short-run financing problem would remain. [1]

The serious financial problem facing the social security system is a relatively recent phenomenon. During the 1950s and 1960s, cash benefits increased tremendously as more people retired, the Disability Insurance program was established, and a series of congressional initiatives extended coverage and liberalized benefits. By 1970, annual OASDI benefits had grown to $33.1 billion, or 8.1 percent of taxable payroll. As shown in table 1, however, the benefit increases were matched by payroll tax hikes, which were made affordable by rapid economic growth, large gains in real wages, and low unemployment. As a result, assets in the OASI and DI trust funds at the beginning of each calendar year exceeded the year's full amount of benefit outlays; that is, their trust fund ratios exceeded 100 percent (see table 2). In addition, since the Medicare program was established under the social security umbrella in 1965, HI payroll taxes have been set at rates that would keep pace with projected Medicare disbursements.

A series of planned and unplanned events in the 1970s jeopardized the financial well-being of the social security system, shattered the public image of the program, and saddled current policy makers with a major economic dilemma. Congress increased social security cash benefits by 15 percent effective January 1970, by 10 percent in January 1971, and by 20 percent under the Social Security Amendments of 1972. The 1972 amend-

3

TABLE 1

Social Security Outlays, Outlays as a Percentage of Taxable Payroll, and Payroll Tax Rates, Selected Calendar Years 1950–1981

Calendar Year	Social Security Outlays (billions of dollars)				Outlays as a Percentage of Taxable Payroll				Payroll Tax Rate[a] (percent)			
	OASI	DI	OASDI	HI	OASI	DI	OASDI	HI	OASI	DI	OASDI	HI
1950	1.0	—	1.0	—	1.17	—	1.17	—	3.0	—	3.0	—
1955	5.1	—	5.1	—	3.34	—	3.34	—	4.0	—	4.0	—
1960	11.2	0.6	11.8	—	5.59	0.30	5.89	—	5.5	0.5	6.0	—
1965	17.5	1.7	19.2	—	7.23	0.70	7.93	—	6.75	0.5	7.25	—
1970	29.8	3.3	33.1	5.3	7.32	0.81	8.12	1.21	7.3	1.1	8.4	1.2
1971	34.5	4.0	38.5	5.9	8.27	0.97	9.23	1.33	8.1	1.1	9.2	1.2
1972	38.5	4.8	43.3	6.5	8.12	1.01	9.13	1.31	8.1	1.1	9.2	1.2
1973	47.2	6.0	53.1	7.3	8.58	1.09	9.68	1.34	8.6	1.1	9.7	2.0
1974	53.4	7.2	60.6	9.4	8.57	1.16	9.73	1.42	8.75	1.15	9.9	1.8
1975	60.4	8.8	69.2	11.6	9.29	1.36	10.65	1.69	8.75	1.15	9.9	1.8
1976	67.9	10.4	78.2	13.7	9.42	1.44	10.86	1.83	8.75	1.15	9.9	1.8
1977	75.3	11.9	87.3	16.0	9.47	1.50	10.97	1.95	8.75	1.15	9.9	1.8
1978	83.1	13.0	96.0	18.2	9.30	1.45	10.75	2.07	8.55	1.55	10.1	2.0
1979	93.1	14.2	107.3	21.1	8.95	1.36	10.31	2.00	8.66	1.5	10.16	2.1
1980	107.7	15.9	123.6	25.6	9.39	1.38	10.77	2.19	9.04	1.12	10.16	2.1
1981[b]	127.0	18.1	145.1	29.6	9.89	1.41	11.30	2.27	9.4	1.30	10.7	2.6

[a] Tax rate is combined employee and employer contributions as a percentage of taxable wages.

[b] Estimated in the 1981 trustees' projection path II-A.

SOURCES: For OASI and DI, Board of Trustees, Federal Old-Age and Survivors Insurance and Disability Insurance Trust Funds, *1981 Annual Report,* 1981, pp. 8, 44, 47, 49, 51; for HI, Board of Trustees, Federal Hospital Insurance Trust Fund, *1981 Annual Report,* 1981, pp. 12, 25, 35.

4

TABLE 2

Fund Assets at Beginning of Year as a Percentage of Expenditures during the Year for OASI, DI, and HI Trust Funds, Selected Calendar Years 1950–1981

Calendar Year	OASI	DI	OASDI	HI
1950	1,156	—	1,156	—
1955	405	—	405	—
1960	180	304	186	—
1965	109	121	110	—
1970	101	126	103	47
1971	94	140	99	54
1972	88	140	93	47
1973	75	125	80	40
1974	68	110	73	69
1975	63	92	66	79
1976	54	71	57	77
1977	47	48	47	66
1978	39	26	37	57
1979	30	30	30	54
1980	23	35	24	52
1981 [a]	18	20 [b]	18	46

[a] Estimated in the 1981 trustees' projection path II-A.

[b] The 1980 trustees estimated this ratio to be 44 percent. It is much lower because of the legislated transfer of funds from the DI fund into OASI.

SOURCES: For OASI and DI, *1981 Annual Report*, pp. 41, 114; for HI, *1981 Annual Report*, p. 38.

ments also included three other provisions that increased benefits. First, social security benefits were indexed to percentage increases in the Consumer Price Index (CPI) effective in 1975. Second, the maximum wage base covered by social security was raised faster than the growth of average covered wages from 1973 to 1975, and it was indexed to lagged increases in average covered wages in the following years (see table 3).[2] This increased trust fund incomes by raising the taxable portion of covered earnings, but it also increased future benefit obligations. Third, the marginal benefit rates in the benefit formula were indexed to the CPI. (This indexing flaw, which has been thoroughly analyzed elsewhere, was corrected by the 1977 amendments.)[3]

Automatically indexed social security cash benefits increased at the same time that the growth of covered wages and of trust fund incomes was slowed by unanticipated high levels of unemployment and low real wage gains. In addition, in response to higher unemployment rates and lower

5

TABLE 3

CHANGES IN THE SOCIAL SECURITY TAX BASE, SELECTED YEARS 1955–1982

Calendar Year	Tax Base (dollars) (1)	Ratio of Taxable Earnings Base to Average Covered Wages (2)	Ratio of Taxable Earnings to Total Covered Earnings[a] (3)
1955	4,200	1.46	.803
1960	4,800	1.36	.781
1965	4,800	1.16	.713
1970	7,800	1.42	.782
1971	7,800	1.36	.763
1972	9,000	1.46	.783
1973	10,800	1.64	.818
1974	13,200	1.86	.853
1975	14,100	1.87	.845
1976	15,300	1.88	.841
1977	16,500	1.89	.835
1978	17,700	1.88	.840
1979	22,900	2.22	.879
1980	25,900	2.31	.884
1981	29,700	2.41[b]	.892[b]
1982	32,100[b]	2.37[b]	.890[b]

[a] Earnings include wages plus self-employed income. The ratio of taxable to covered wages is higher than those figures shown.

[b] Estimated, based on the Reagan administration's *Fiscal Year 1982 Budget Revisions*, March 1981.

SOURCES: Column 2, Frank deLeeuw and others, "The High-Employment Budget: New Estimates, 1955-80," *Survey of Current Business*, vol. 60, no. 11 (November 1980), pp. 13–43. Column 3, U.S. Congress, Senate, Subcommittee on Social Security of the Committee on Finance, *Staff Data and Materials Related to Social Security Financing*, 97th Congress, 1st session, February 1980, table 55, pp. 86–87; and Ken Sander, Office of Research and Statistics, Social Security Administration.

real wage gains and to high social security benefits that were both tax exempt and protected from inflation, more workers than expected began to retire early and collect OASI benefits. DI eligibility rolls also continued to grow.[4] The decline in the worker-to-beneficiary ratio, coupled with the generous benefit increases, accelerated the erosion of the combined OASDI trust fund assets, from 66 percent of annual expenditures at the beginning of 1975 to 47 percent in 1977. Simultaneously, although Medicare entitlements automatically kept pace with soaring medical costs, they were matched by a sizable HI payroll tax hike in 1973. The HI fund was not projected to be exhausted until the mid-1980s.[5]

Before the 1977 amendments, OASI and DI benefits were projected to exceed payroll taxes in every year through 1981, when trust funds would reach insolvent levels.[6] In addition, the indexing flaw of the 1972 amendments required early attention. Congress was forced to tackle the financing issue. It resolved the long-run problem caused by the indexing flaw by changing the benefit formula and indexing both earnings histories and the benefit brackets ("bend points") to changes in average wages.[7] This adjustment lowered long-term benefit projections but still provided future retirees generous increases in real benefits.[8] Congress ignored the long-run financial deficit caused by demographic shifts and, except for implementing a few minor cuts, opted to raise payroll taxes to close the projected short-run gap between benefits and taxes.[9] Payroll tax rates were increased, particularly those earmarked for DI and HI, while a provision that superseded the automatic adjustment of the taxable wage base for 1979 through 1981 raised the wage base from $17,700 in 1978 to $29,700 in 1981. As a result, from 1978 to 1981, the ratio of taxable to total covered earnings increased from .840 to .892, and the ratio of the taxable earnings base to average covered wages grew from 1.88 to 2.41. Congress rejected proposals to fund social security from general revenues and agreed to continue assessing payroll taxes equally on employers and employees.

NOTES TO CHAPTER 2

[1] See National Commission on Social Security, *Social Security in America's Future*, March 1981, p. 81; Congressional Budget Office, *Paying for Social Security: Funding Options for the Near Term*, February 1981, pp. 13, 20; and Board of Trustees, Federal Old-Age and Survivors Insurance, Disability Insurance, and Hospital Insurance Trust Funds, *1981 Annual Report*, 1981.

[2] Specifically, the taxable maximum wage base was escalated in proportion to the first-quarter-over-first-quarter increase in average wages, lagged two years, with increases rounded to the nearest $300 increment. (It is now indexed to year-over-year increases in average wages, lagged two years.)

[3] See, for example, Colin D. Campbell, *Over-Indexed Benefits: The Decoupling Proposals for Social Security* (Washington, D.C.: American Enterprise Institute, 1976), and Lawrence H. Thompson, "Toward the Rational Adjustment of Social Security Benefit Levels," *Policy Analysis*, vol. 3 (Fall 1977), pp. 485–508.

[4] For a discussion of factors that affect the retirement decision, see Robert L. Clark and David T. Barker, *Reversing the Trend toward Early Retirement* (Washington, D.C.: American Enterprise Institute, 1981). See also Paul Van de Water, "Disability Insurance," *Papers and Proceedings of the Ninety-first Annual Meeting of the American Economic Association*, May 1979, pp. 275–78, and Darwin

7

Johnson, *The Sensitivity of Federal Expenditures to Unemployment,* Office of Management and Budget, Technical Staff Paper, April 18, 1980.

[5] U.S. Congress, Senate, Committee on Finance, *Staff Data and Materials Relating to Social Security Financing,* 95th Congress, 1st session, June 1977, p. 37.

[6] U.S. Senate, Committee on Finance, *Staff Data and Materials Relating to Social Security Financing,* June 1977, pp. 18–19.

[7] This includes all wages, including those earned in noncovered employment. As is discussed in appendix A, however, the effect on the benefits of new recipients of the 1972 indexing flaw will not be completely eliminated until 1984.

[8] See William C. Hsiao, "An Optimal Indexing Method for Social Security," and Robert S. Kaplan, "A Comparison of Rates of Return to Social Security Retirees under Wage and Price Indexing," in Colin D. Campbell, ed., *Financing Social Security* (Washington, D.C.: American Enterprise Institute, 1979), pp. 19–40, 119–44.

[9] See Colin D. Campbell, *The 1977 Amendments to the Social Security Act* (Washington, D.C.: American Enterprise Institute, 1978).

3

The Short-Run Financing Issue since 1977

In 1978, the acting commissioner of social security stated: "With the signing of the Social Security Amendments of 1977 into law, the Congress and the President have assured the financial soundness of the social security program for the next 50 years."[1] This optimism was reflected in the trustees' *1978 Annual Report,* which projected a rapid turnaround of trust fund balances and a surplus through 2027. The *1979 Annual Report* and the 1979 report of the Advisory Council were only slightly more pessimistic. They projected the combined OASDI trust fund ratio to fall from 30 percent in 1979 to 25 percent in 1980 and to a low of 22 percent in 1981, but to rebound thereafter, climbing continuously to safe levels into the next century. Even under the trustees' pessimistic assumptions in 1979, the combined OASDI trust funds ratio was projected to decline to only 18 percent in 1981 and to 16 percent in 1982, levels that were certainly not comforting by historical standards, but were still adequate under most circumstances to finance scheduled benefits throughout the year. (Because social security benefits are disbursed at the beginning of each month while payroll taxes are collected over the entire month, financial solvency is threatened when trust fund ratios at the beginning of any calendar year fall below 9 percent.)[2]

The projected margins of financial safety provided by the 1977 amendments eroded quickly, however, because of unanticipated high rates of unemployment and inflation and declines in real wages. In 1978 and 1979, the growth of trust fund incomes fell below anticipated levels as the unemployment rate averaged 6.0 percent and 5.8 percent, respectively, and as the real wage differential—that is, the percentage increase in average covered wages minus the percentage increase in average annual CPI—increased by 0.5 percent and then declined by 3.1 percent.[3] At the same time, inflation accelerated and social security OASDI benefits rose automatically in June of those years by 9.9 percent and 14.3 percent. The substantial increases in HI payroll taxes allowed balances in the HI fund to remain above 50 percent, despite rises in Medicare outlays.

Benefiting from hindsight and basing projections on dismal short-run prognoses of the economy, the National Commission on Social Security (NCSS) and the Congressional Budget Office (CBO) released reports in early 1981 that erased any remaining optimism regarding the short-term financing picture.[4] The reports projected that the OASI trust fund would be inadequate in 1983. Combining the OASI and DI funds in an attempt to bail out the troubled OASI fund would not ensure solvency beyond 1983, while enlisting the aid of HI funds would not ensure solvency of the combined funds beyond 1984.

Table 4 displays trust fund ratios estimated by several recent reports under their "intermediate assumptions."[5] The trustees' *1981 Annual Report* includes five short-run projection paths; the path displayed, path II-A, is nearly identical with the economic assumptions published by the Reagan administration in its March 1981 budget revisions for fiscal year 1982. The trust fund ratios in each of the projections and the economic assumptions of the projections are shown in appendix B.

TABLE 4

ESTIMATED TRUST FUND RATIOS FOR SOCIAL SECURITY AND HOSPITAL
INSURANCE PROGRAMS, CALENDAR YEARS 1980–1985

(percent)

Fund/Source of Estimate	1980	1981	1982	1983	1984	1985
OASI[a]						
1979 trustees and						
Advisory Council	24	19	17	18	18	18
1980 trustees	23	15	6	—2	—10	—17
NCSS	23	17	10	1	—10	—20
1981 trustees	23	18	13	5	—4	—13
DI[a]						
1979 trustees and						
Advisory Council	25	25	32	n.a.	n.a.	n.a.
1980 trustees	35	44	61	83	111	142
NCSS	35	20	12	30	52	79
1981 trustees	35	20	13	33	62	96
OASDI						
1979 trustees and						
Advisory Council	25	22	23	26	29	32
1980 trustees	24	18	12	8	4	0
NCSS	24	18	10	4	—3	—9
1981 trustees	24	18	13	8	3	—1
HI						
1979 trustees and						
Advisory Council	53	51	64	73	77	76
1980 trustees	53	52	65	76	82	84
NCSS	54	52	64	73	79	83
1981 trustees	52	46	57	66	70	70

TABLE 4 (continued)

Fund/Source of Estimate	1980	1981	1982	1983	1984	1985
OASDHI						
1979 trustees and						
Advisory Council	n.a.	n.a.	n.a.	n.a.	n.a.	n.a.
1980 trustees	29	24	21	19	18	16
NCSS	29	23	19	16	12	8
1981 trustees	29	23	21	18	15	13

NOTES: Trust fund ratio is assets in the fund at the beginning of the year as a percentage of total benefit outlays in the year. Projections are based on intermediate assumptions of each source and path II-A of the 1981 trustees' report. Path II-A is nearly identical with the Reagan administration's economic projections published in Executive Office of the President, *Fiscal Year 1982 Budget Revisions,* March 1981. n.a. = not available.

a The separate trust fund ratios for OASI and DI estimated by the 1979 and 1980 trustees, on the one hand, and the NCSS and 1981 trustees, on the other, are not directly comparable because the 1979 and 1980 trustees' projections do not include the effect of the 1980 amendments, which reallocated DI tax rate receipts to the OASI fund in 1980 and 1981.

SOURCES: Board of Trustees, Federal Old-Age and Survivors Insurance, Disability Insurance, and Hospital Insurance Trust Funds, *1980 Annual Report,* 1980, p. 90, and *1981 Annual Report,* 1981, pp. 114–15; U.S. Department of Health, Education and Welfare, Advisory Council on Social Security, *Social Security Financing and Benefits,* December 1979, p. 33; and National Commission on Social Security, *Social Security in America's Future,* March 1981, p. 81.

The accuracy of these projections depends, of course, on their underlying assumptions. The NCSS intermediate projections are based on economic assumptions that are more pessimistic than those of the Reagan administration and path II-A of the 1981 trustees' report.[6] Table 5 compares these two sets of assumptions. The NCSS projections assume higher unemployment rates, particularly through 1983, and slower growth of real gross national product (GNP). Annual percentage changes in average wages in covered employment are similar in the two projections. In 1981, the NCSS assumes no change in real wages, while the Reagan administration assumes a higher rate of inflation and a slight decline in real wages. After 1981, however, the Reagan administration assumes a much lower rate of inflation than the NCSS and, as a result, substantially higher gains in real wages. From 1982 to 1986, the real wage differential is roughly twice as high under the Reagan administration's projections. If the economy rebounds according to the Reagan administration's more optimistic projections, the OASI and combined OASDI would reach insolvent levels in 1983, but the combined OASDI plus Medicare (HI) trust funds would remain solvent until early 1985, when the fund ratio would be 13 percent. On the other hand, if the assumed improvements in real wage gains are not realized, any hope for financial solvency will deteriorate. For example, if real wages remain roughly constant (as is assumed in the pessimistic path III of the 1981 trustees' report), the combined OASDHI funds would reach insolvent levels before the end of 1983.

TABLE 5

Comparison of Major Economic Assumptions of the NCSS Intermediate Projections and the Reagan Administration and 1981 Trustees' Path II-A Projections, Calendar Years 1980–1986

Economic Assumption and Source of Estimate	1980	1981	1982	1983	1984	1985	1986
Real GNP (annual percent change)							
NCSS	−1.4	0.3	3.8	4.2	4.3	4.3	3.7
Reagan administration and 1981 trustees' path II-A	−0.1ᵃ	1.1	4.2	5.0	4.5	4.2	4.2
CPI (annual percent change)							
NCSS	13.4	9.7	8.9	7.8	6.9	6.2	6.0
Reagan administration and 1981 trustees' path II-A	13.5ᵃ	11.1	8.3	6.2	5.5	4.7	4.2
Average wages in covered employment (annual percent change)							
NCSS	8.6	9.7	9.8	8.6	8.0	7.5	7.4
Reagan administration and 1981 trustees' path II-Aᵇ	8.5ᵃ	10.4	9.8	8.8	7.9	7.1	7.0
Real wage differential (percentage points)ᶜ							
NCSS	−4.8	0.0	0.9	0.8	1.1	1.3	1.4
Reagan administration and 1981 trustees' path II-Aᵈ	−5.0ᵃ	−0.7	1.5	2.6	2.4	2.4	2.8
Unemployment rate (percent)							
NCSS	7.6	8.5	8.0	7.3	5.6	6.0	5.7
Reagan administration and 1981 trustees' path II-Aᵉ	7.2ᵃ	7.8	7.2	6.6	6.4	6.0	5.6

ᵃ Actual figures.

ᵇ These figures are not published in the budget but are consistent with the Reagan administration's projections that appear in the *Fiscal Year 1982 Budget Revisions*, except that the 1981 trustees' path II-A projection assumes average covered wages will increase by 10.2 percent in 1981 and 8.6 percent in 1983.

ᶜ The difference between the percentage increase in average annual covered wages and the percentage increase in the average annual CPI.

ᵈ The 1981 trustees' path II-A projection assumes real wage differentials of 0.9 in 1981 and 2.4 in 1983.

ᵉ The 1981 trustees' path II-A projection assumes a 5.9 percent unemployment rate in 1985.

Sources: *Social Security in America's Future*, p. 80; Executive Office of the President, *Fiscal Year 1982 Budget Revisions*, March 1981, p. 13; Social Security Administration, Office of Research and Statistics, and *1981 Annual Report*, p. 29.

12

The trust fund balances are very sensitive to economic conditions. At fiscal year 1981 levels, a one-percentage-point increase in the unemployment rate would reduce payroll tax receipts by $3.4 billion, while a one-percentage-point increase in the inflation rate would add approximately $1.4 billion of cash benefits because of the automatic adjustment of benefits.[7] These estimates do not include the effect of higher rates of unemployment or inflation in encouraging early retirement or increasing disability insurance rolls.

NOTES TO CHAPTER 3

[1] John Shee and Mary Ross, "Social Security Amendments of 1977: Legislative History and Summary of Provisions," *Social Security Bulletin,* March 1978, p. 4.

[2] In the light of normal cyclical behavior in the economy, the 1981 trustees state that trust fund ratios of 14 percent should be maintained in order to ensure solvency. Board of Trustees, Federal Old-Age and Survivors Insurance, Disability Insurance, and Hospital Insurance Trust Funds, *1981 Annual Report,* 1981, appendix C, pp. 91–98.

What does it mean to say that the assets in a trust fund have run dry? The social security programs are funded on a pay-as-you-go basis, with the trust funds providing a cushion in case current benefit disbursements exceed current trust fund income. Because scheduled OASI benefits are expected to exceed income during each of the next several years, the trust fund would be depleted, and thus the full amount of scheduled benefits could not be disbursed. Even if Congress did not take action, however, current payroll taxes could fund nearly all of the benefits that would be paid under solvent conditions—approximately 94 percent of the scheduled OASI benefit would be paid in 1983.

[3] As defined in the annual reports of the trustees of the Social Security Administration, average covered wages equal the sum of all wages earned by workers in covered employment divided by the number of workers in covered employment. The number of workers is not adjusted for hours (or days) worked. The "real wage differential" is a commonly used term in the annual reports.

[4] National Commission on Social Security, *Social Security in America's Future,* March 1981; Congressional Budget Office, *Paying for Social Security: Funding Options for the Near Term,* February 1981.

[5] The CBO projections, which are somewhat more pessimistic than the NCSS projections, are not shown because they are reported for fiscal years rather than calendar years.

[6] The NCSS assumptions are based on a blend of the 1980 trustees' assumptions and projections in Executive Office of the President, *Mid-Session Review of the Fiscal Year 1981 Budget,* July 21, 1980.

[7] Inflation reduces trust fund assets if real taxable wages decline. Even if wages keep pace with inflation, trust fund assets as a percentage of annual outlays decline in response to inflation.

4

SHORT-RUN OPTIONS FOR FINANCING SOCIAL SECURITY

In 1981, Congress faces a much different economic and political climate than existed before the 1977 amendments. There is uncertainty about the persistence of recent unfavorable economic conditions such as low productivity and declining real wages, coupled with high rates of inflation and unemployment. In addition, there is a strong trend toward federal fiscal austerity. In its March 1981 *Fiscal Year 1982 Budget Revisions,* the Reagan administration proposed—and the Congress has supported—large cuts in nondefense programs other than social security. In May 1981, the administration followed with a major social security reform package that included large cuts in benefits.[1] Although the immediate congressional response to this reform package (particularly the provision to reduce benefits for early retirees) was strongly negative, there is a growing belief that future social security benefits should be trimmed for broad fiscal reasons as well as to preserve the solvency of the trust funds.

Ways to resolve the short-run financing problem fall into three general categories. The first includes methods that would not reduce benefits or increase payroll taxes, but instead would reallocate funds, either within the social security system or within the context of the entire federal budget. The second category involves increasing payroll taxes, and the third involves reducing benefit levels. As described below, the funds reallocation approach should not be relied upon alone because it will not achieve financial solvency through the 1980s unless the growth in real wages increases substantially and, in any case, such a strategy would delay consideration of how to deal with the long-run actuarial deficit.

FUNDS REALLOCATION APPROACH

Reallocating the OASI, DI, and HI tax rates, combining the funds, or allowing interfund borrowing may resolve, or at least postpone, the short-run financing issue since the OASI fund is being depleted more rapidly than either the DI or the HI fund. One limitation to this approach is that the DI and HI programs are much smaller than the OASI program.

The NCSS estimated that increasing the portion of payroll taxes earmarked for the OASI fund and reducing the amount for DI would postpone trust fund exhaustion only several months, while shifting a portion of HI payroll taxes into the OASI fund would delay insolvency less than one year.[2] Merging the OASI, DI, and HI trust funds and reallocating payroll taxes would keep the OASI fund afloat only two years longer than otherwise. Approximately the same results would occur if interfund borrowing were allowed.

Whether reallocation of trust funds and income payroll taxes would be a sufficient short-run solution depends on the performance of the economy. The funds would be exhausted earlier if, for example, productivity and real wage growth continued to decline or remained low over the next several years. If, instead, real wage growth rises beginning in 1982 as the Reagan administration anticipates, the interfund reallocation approach would resolve the short-run financing problem. Hoping for a turnaround in real wage growth and dealing with any financial problem at the last possible moment seem irresponsible, however, and may lead to an undesirable, "quick-fix" policy.

A second type of fund reallocation to resolve the short-run financing problem would be to allow the social security trust funds to borrow as needed from the Treasury or to provide general fund financing, as a one-shot injection, as periodic injections triggered by an economic indicator such as the unemployment rate, or as an ongoing process. The standard argument in support of financing social security in part from general revenues is that, besides bailing out the system, it would reduce the regressive burden of payroll taxes. This argument is weakened, however, by two considerations. First, the highly graduated benefit structure, which replaces a higher percentage of preretirement earnings for lower-income workers than for higher-income workers, more than outweighs the regressive burden of payroll taxes.[3] Second, the earned income credit (EIC), available to low-income earners with dependent children, is now tied directly to payroll taxes by a provision that allows an eligible EIC recipient to receive advance payments from employers to offset all or part of the payroll tax burden in each paycheck.[4] As such, it operates as a means-tested personal exemption by reducing the effective payroll tax burden for low-income earners. Another argument in support of financing social security with general revenues instead of payroll taxes is that it would lessen inflationary pressures. Although this financing shift might have a desirable short-run impact on the CPI, it would have no long-run effect on inflation if the employers' share of payroll taxes were borne entirely by employees, or if deficits added to inflationary pressures, regardless of their source.

Several arguments have been raised against shifting to general revenue financing, which, of course, would change only the source and not the total tax burden for social security. Opponents usually argue that it would loosen the link between a participant's contributions and benefits. If higher income taxes were substituted for payroll taxes so that benefits were in no way tied to

15

taxes, then workers would perceive payments to social security as taxes rather than as a form of mandatory saving.[5] This would have disincentive effects on labor supply. In addition, people may be less disposed to higher taxes than to mandatory saving. Also, it has been argued that general fund financing would lead to fiscal irresponsibility (benefit expansions) by Congress, could result in means tests for certain benefits, and would only add to the size of the deficit.[6] In terms of policy making, the infusion of general funds might give Congress a false sense of accomplishment and would only delay meaningful financing reform of the system.

Removing Medicare from payroll tax financing, either partially or entirely, has merit and should be considered as a long-run goal. It has been recommended by the majority of the members of the 1975 and 1979 Advisory Councils and the National Commission on Social Security. The supporting argument is that, unlike OASI and DI benefits, Medicare benefits are not related to a participant's earnings. The arguments against shifting the funding source of Medicare are the same as those against any type of general fund financing of social security. In addition, although Medicare benefits are unrelated to earnings, some fear that removing Medicare from social security would eliminate its only link to "insurance" and might allow it to be gradually changed to a means-tested program.

Removing Medicare from payroll tax financing has been considered as a means of circumventing the short-run OASI financing problem. Resolving the short-run financing problem of OASI by reallocating all or part of HI taxes to OASI and financing Medicare from general revenues would, however, be a mistake.[7] While removing Medicare from social security is desirable, it should be considered on its own merit and should not be confused with the OASI financing problem. The removal of Medicare from social security should begin only after the OASI and DI programs have been put on a sound financial basis.

RAISING PAYROLL TAXES

Projected short-run deficits may be eliminated by increasing payroll taxes, either by higher tax rates or by a higher taxable wage base. The Congressional Budget Office estimates that a one-percentage-point increase in the payroll tax rate above the scheduled level would generate an additional $80 billion in tax revenues in fiscal years 1982–1986.[8] This amount would maintain solvency of the OASI trust fund (under the CBO's projections) if all of the additional revenues were allotted to OASI. Increasing the payroll tax rate would distribute the additional tax burden among workers in proportion to their taxable earnings. An increase of one percentage point (one-half assessed on employees and one-half on employers) would initially increase the share paid by employees and employers by $50 a year for each $10,000 in covered wages, or a maximum of $148.50 annually in 1981 for workers earning

$29,700 or more. Opponents of this approach contend that increasing a proportional tax would increase the regressivity of the total tax burden.

Eliminating the maximum wage base and subjecting all covered wages to the payroll tax would yield approximately $40 billion more in payroll taxes in fiscal years 1982–1986, according to the CBO.[9] This would place the entire burden of the payroll tax increase on higher-income workers. At 1981 levels, a worker earning $45,000 would face an annual increase of more than 50 percent, from $1,975 to $2,992, while the payroll taxes of a worker earning $59,400 would double. Increasing the taxable maximum would also raise the average indexed monthly earnings (AIME) of high-income workers and would increase future benefit obligations to them. Because of the highly graduated benefit schedule, however, in which the marginal benefit rate applicable to persons with high AIMEs is only 15 percent, the additional benefit received by higher-income participants would be less than their increase in payroll taxes. This would greatly increase the intragenerational redistribution of wealth through the social security program. In addition, others argue that increasing the wage base displaces the growth of funds in private pensions and further dampens personal saving. Both the 1979 Advisory Council and the NCSS have recommended slowing the rise in the taxable maximum.[10]

Historically, scheduled social security benefits in general have been considered sacrosanct, and trust fund solvency has been achieved by adjusting payroll taxes upward as necessary to finance scheduled benefit levels. Relying entirely on higher taxes to close the projected short-term gap between social security benefits and taxes, and to restore trust fund balances to safe levels, would perpetuate the traditional approach to social security financing. It might create more problems than it solved. Insofar as raising payroll taxes reduced disposable income and dampened the rate of personal saving, it would offset some of the intended consequences of the personal income tax cuts proposed by the Reagan administration and enacted in 1981. In addition, it would allow social security benefits to continue growing unabated.

TRIMMING BENEFITS

Until recently, the question of the affordability of the level of current and future benefits provided by existing law was rarely addressed.[11] This one-sided approach was a mistake; neither benefits nor taxes should be ignored or taken as given. The emphasis is now changing, as the Reagan administration and several key members of Congress have proposed major social security financing reforms that include selective benefit cuts.[12] Selective cutbacks of benefits that are excessive or redundant would be a constructive start toward eliminating the program's actuarial imbalance. The financial impact of any short-term cutbacks would accumulate over time.

Before discussing individual cuts, we need first to consider the present

17

size and distribution of benefits. According to the Reagan budget, under current law, OASDI benefits in fiscal year 1981 will be $137.8 billion, or 21.0 percent of total federal outlays; that portion is projected to grow to 23.3 percent by fiscal year 1986.[13] The largest portion of benefits is disbursed to low-income recipients who rely on social security benefits for the majority of their money income. In 1978, the last year for which distributional information is available, slightly over half of all recipients had total income, including social security benefits, of less than $7,000, as shown in table 6.[14] Some recipients, however, have substantial income from other sources. In 1978, nearly 16 percent of all recipients had total incomes exceeding $15,000, and they received nearly 21 percent of all benefits. More than 5 percent of all recipients must be considered well-off—they had total income over $25,000. (Recipients have substantially more income—in nominal dollars—today than they did in 1978). These figures indicate that social security has gone well beyond its intent of providing a floor of income security for the aged, retired, and disabled, and suggest that there is some room for cuts that would not jeopardize the financial well-being of the program recipients.

The original Reagan budget proposal included only four minor changes that would reduce social security benefits: eliminate the social security legal minimum benefit, eliminate social security benefits for adult students, eliminate the lump-sum death benefit where there are no surviving family members, and tighten eligibility for disability insurance.[15] That was followed in May 1981 by a much more comprehensive reform package, which had two goals: to achieve financial soundness in the system by slowing the growth in benefits, and to provide incentives that would slow the trend toward early retirement.[16]

Table 7 displays estimates of the effect on benefits of seven proposals that would not change the way the primary insurance amount (PIA) is calculated. (The PIA is the initial benefit to a new retiree; it is the basis from which actuarial reductions or increases are made for early or delayed retirement and from which dependents' and survivors' benefits are calculated.) The table indicates whether the same proposal or one similar in intent is included in the Reagan administration proposals or in H.R. 3207 or has been recommended in other recent official reports. Several other major reforms are discussed in chapter 5, which considers the long-run financing issue.[17]

Student Benefits. Student benefits are one of several social security benefit programs that should be seriously considered for eventual elimination. Benefits are now available to full-time postsecondary students who are unmarried and between the ages of eighteen and twenty-two, whose parents are social security recipients (benefits paid to dependent children normally end on a child's eighteenth birthday). The Reagan administration has recommended phasing out these benefits. In March 1981, 898,000 students—about one-ninth of all eighteen- to twenty-one-year-olds enrolled full time—received an average monthly benefit of $222 ($2,659 on an annual basis).[18] The benefits are based

TABLE 6

Social Security Recipients and Benefits by Income Level in 1978

Income Level[a] (dollars)	Number of Recipients[b] (thousands)	Percentage of Total Recipients[c]	Percentage of Total Benefits Distributed	Average Benefit per Recipient (dollars)
Below 0[d]	131	0.38	0.32	3,014
0–3,000	6,968	20.14	10.51	1,878
3,000–5,000	6,989	20.20	17.76	3,161
5,000–7,000	4,657	13.46	14.10	3,764
7,000–10,000	5,263	15.21	17.59	4,158
10,000–15,000	5,079	14.68	18.79	4,599
15,000–20,000	2,391	6.91	9.23	4,805
20,000–25,000	1,235	3.57	4.41	4,439
25,000–30,000	716	2.07	2.66	4,631
30,000–50,000	799	2.31	3.13	4,868
Over 50,000	381	1.10	1.48	4,866
Total[e] or average	34,600	100.00	100.00	3,594

[a] The income level equals adjusted gross income plus social security benefits plus preference items included in the minimum tax base, such as the excluded portion of capital gains.

[b] These figures are calculated by multiplying the percentage of total number of beneficiaries (as calculated in the Treasury Tax Model) by 34.6 million, the total number of OASDI recipients in 1978.

[c] The precise definition of this column is percentage of tax-filing units that had social security benefits.

[d] Includes all social security beneficiaries who reported negative income.

[e] Detail may not add to totals because of rounding.

Source: Based on the U.S. Department of the Treasury's Personal Individual Income Tax Model, 1978 income levels, and 1978 social security benefit schedules. Included in social security benefits are Old-Age and Survivors Insurance (OASI) and Disability Insurance (DI), plus railroad retirement. Health Insurance (Medicare) benefits are not included. Reprinted from Mickey D. Levy, *The Tax Treatment of Social Security* (Washington, D.C.: American Enterprise Institute, 1980), pp. 8–9.

TABLE 7

ESTIMATED IMPACT ON NET BENEFITS OF SOCIAL SECURITY PROPOSALS, FISCAL YEARS 1982–1986
(millions of dollars)

Proposal[a]	1982	1983	1984	1985	1986	Total
Phase out student benefit (1,2,4[b])	−650	−1,235	−1,820	−2,480	−2,710	−8,895
Phase out survivor benefit for parents of children aged 16 and 17 (2,4[b])	−25	−90	−500	−525	−535	−1,675
Eliminate minimum benefit (1[c],2,3[d],4)	−65	−135	−160	−205	−225	−790
Eliminate lump-sum death benefit (1[e])	−400	−410	−420	−435	−450	−2,115
Phase out retirement test between 1983 and 1986 (1,2,4)	0	500	1,100	1,600	2,600	5,800
Tax benefits that exceed contributions[f] (4[g],5)	−10,275	−12,010	−14,050	−16,420	−19,160	−71,915
Change the indexation of benefits (3[h])			uncertain			
Total (excluding indexing change)	−11,415	−13,380	−15,850	−18,465	−20,480	−79,590

[a] The numbers alongside each proposal indicate whether it (or a proposal similar in intent) has been proposed by the following:
1. the Reagan administration
2. Congressman J. J. Pickle (H.R. 3207)
3. National Commission on Social Security
4. President's Commission on Pension Policy
5. 1979 Advisory Council

[b] The President's Commission on Pension Policy recommends that this provision be reexamined "and put on a more rational basis."

[c] The Reagan administration would complement the elimination of the minimum benefit with a pension offset in an attempt to eliminate the windfall benefits for persons who also receive pensions for noncovered earnings.

[d] The NCSS would eliminate the windfall benefits by including an individual's noncovered earnings (up to the taxable maximum) in the calculations of his or her primary insurance amount.

[e] The Reagan administration would eliminate lump-sum death benefits when there are no surviving family members. This would save roughly one-half of the figures shown.

[f] Taxing benefits that exceed contributions would reduce net benefits by increasing personal income taxes rather than by reducing benefit disbursements from the social security trust funds. For simplicity, these calculations assume that, for the average social security recipient in 1982 to 1986, lifetime contributions constitute 25 percent of benefits. Contributions as a percentage of benefits would be higher for higher-income earners and multiple-earner households with earnings greater than the taxable maximum, but would be lower for workers with lower earnings histories. The actual average percentage may be lower for persons already retired. The percentage is expected to increase over time because of higher expected payroll taxes.

[g] The President's Commission on Pension Policy would allow all payroll taxes to be deductible and would tax all benefits when received.

[h] The NCSS would index benefits by the lower of the percentage increases in wages or prices, but would allow a catch-up of real benefits in years when real wages rise.

SOURCES: All of the figures except for the impact of phasing out the retirement test and taxing benefits that exceed contributions are from Congressional Budget Office, *Paying for Social Security: Funding Options for the Near Term*, February 1981, table 9, p. 33. The impact of phasing out the retirement test as proposed by the Reagan administration is from the Social Security Administration, Office of the Actuary. The calculation for taxing benefits that exceed contributions is derived from Joint Committee on Taxation, *Estimates of Federal Tax Expenditures for Fiscal Years 1981–86*, March 16, 1981.

21

on the parents' earnings, with students of higher-earning families receiving more than students of lower-earning families; so the benefits provided tend to be inversely related to need. When student benefits were first established by the Social Security Amendments of 1965, no major federal programs offering grant assistance to students were available. Since then, federal student assistance programs have expanded rapidly, making the social security student benefits poorly targeted and, in many cases, duplicative.[19] If these benefits were phased out, so that no new students would be eligible for the benefits, the low- and middle-income students would be eligible for federal student assistance. Thus, eliminating the student benefits would trim unnecessary benefits and improve the targeting of social security benefits toward the truly needy.

Minimum Benefit. The minimum benefit, which since 1979 has been frozen at $122 a month, was originally intended to provide a floor of cash benefits for retirees with low earnings histories, particularly those with intermittent periods of work in covered employment. Since 1974, however, Supplemental Security Income (SSI) has provided cash benefits to these retirees, with SSI benefits reduced by one dollar for each dollar of social security benefits received in excess of $20 a month. Some of the retirees who receive the minimum benefit are low-income persons whose labor force participation was sporadic. Accordingly, the minimum benefits provided to these persons only replace SSI benefits (except for the $20 a month), so that eliminating the minimum benefit would affect primarily the source but not the level of the cash benefits they receive. A disturbingly large portion of minimum benefits, however, is disbursed to high-income recipients, of whom the largest group are retired civil servants who work in the private sector just long enough to be eligible for social security benefits. This group has low earnings histories in employment covered by social security but generally high incomes from the very generous civil service retirement program and perhaps other sources. Clearly, the benefits provided to these persons under the minimum benefit provision are actually intended for the poor. These windfall benefits are a drain on the social security system, and they could be ended without reducing the cash income of the recipients for whom they are intended.[20]

Some persons who now receive the minimum social security benefit would have to register to receive SSI benefits, which may involve a stigma that is attached to welfare payments. This is unfortunate and may be avoided if the windfall benefits that now accrue to civil service retirees can be ended without eliminating the minimum benefit. (This may be accomplished through a certain form of universal coverage; see chapter 4.)

Lump-Sum Death Benefit. A lump-sum benefit of $255 is paid to surviving families of workers eligible for social security benefits. It was originally intended to pay for a portion of burial costs, and its real value has been eroded by inflation since 1954. In March 1981, 155,540 death benefit payments were disbursed. The Social Security Administration considers it a valuable administrative tool as the "terminal" benefit paid to a participant. Nevertheless, eliminating the lump-sum benefit and replacing it with higher SSI benefits for the truly needy would improve social security financing and target benefits in a more efficient manner.

The Reagan administration would eliminate the lump-sum death benefit when there are no surviving family members. Under current law, when there is neither a spouse nor a child to receive survivor benefits, which occurs in approximately half the cases, the payments go directly to funeral home operators. The administrative costs of these disbursements are very high. The lump-sum payments to survivors would continue under the administration's proposal.

Survivor Benefits for Parents of Children Aged Sixteen and Seventeen. Social security benefits are provided to the surviving parents of children until the children reach age eighteen. The recommendation to phase out these survivor benefits when the dependent turns sixteen is based on the argument that the parents of children aged sixteen and seventeen are not homebound and could seek employment; in fact, the CBO has estimated that roughly half of surviving parents who benefit from this provision are in the work force.[21]

The Social Security Retirement Test. In 1981, the social security retirement test reduces benefits by one dollar for every two dollars of annual wages (or earnings from self-employment) in excess of $5,500 earned by recipients between the ages of sixty-five and seventy-two. (In 1982, it will apply only to annual earnings in excess of $6,000 for recipients between the ages of sixty-five and seventy.)[22] Since the retirement test applies only to income from wages or self-employed earnings, the amount of benefits is not reduced if the recipient has nonwage (so-called unearned) income. Opponents of the retirement test argue that it constitutes an implicit 50 percent tax on wages and thereby encourages early retirement. They contend that it is poor public policy to discourage the elderly from remaining active in the labor market.[23] Two arguments are used to support the retirement test. The first is simply that removing it would be expensive because benefit disbursements would rise. Of course, the costs of removing the retirement test would be reduced to the extent it stimulated higher labor supply by the elderly. Second, some contend that OASI benefits are intended for the retired, and the retirement test determines, at least in part, who is eligible.[24]

The 1975 Advisory Council recommended liberalizing the retirement test by reducing benefits one dollar for every three dollars of wages in excess of the excludable level. The Reagan administration's proposal would phase out the retirement test over a three-year period, permitting $10,000 of wage exclusion in 1983, $15,000 in 1984, $20,000 in 1985, and unlimited thereafter. Although the administration's proposal would be costly, eliminating the retirement test would be a sound policy. It should be complemented, however, by removing the exclusion of benefits from personal income taxes.[25]

Taxing a Portion of Social Security Cash Benefits. The exclusion of social security benefits from personal income taxation provides a financial advantage to high-income recipients (those with income other than social security benefits) by allowing them to pay lower taxes than persons who do not receive social security benefits but have the same total income. Lower-income recipients who receive their total income from social security do not benefit from the tax-exempt status because their income is so low that they would not pay taxes in any event. Viewing the issue from another angle, taxing all or a portion of benefits would not affect lower-income recipients who rely on social security benefits for all or most of their income (over half of all recipients would not be affected), but would reduce net benefits of higher-income recipients in proportion to their marginal tax rate. For example, a couple over sixty-five receiving $7,400 in social security benefits with no other income would be protected by the $3,400 zero bracket amount and the $4,000 in personal exemptions (normal personal exemption plus one additional for the elderly), and they would not have taxable income. Based on 1978 data, fewer than 10 percent of all social security recipients would have incomes high enough for their net benefits to be reduced by more than one-quarter.

The tax-exempt status is a source of sizable revenue losses for the Treasury. Transferring the increased personal income taxes from taxing a portion of benefits back into the social security system would more than pay for eliminating the retirement test and also would resolve the short-run financing problem. One argument against taxing benefits is that current beneficiaries would incur reductions in planned net benefits. However, since wages are a major source of income of recipients who would be affected most by taxing a portion of benefits, removing the tax-exempt status of benefits and eliminating the earnings test should be phased in simultaneously.[26]

The proper tax treatment of social security involves consideration of a worker's lifetime payroll taxes, which are deductible by employers but not by employees and the self-employed, as well as the person's benefits. Accordingly, the current tax treatment could be altered in either of two ways: tax benefits that exceed payroll taxes, analogous to the tax treatment of private pensions; or allow all payroll taxes to be deductible and fully tax benefits, an approach consistent with a comprehensive income tax. Although current Social Security Administration records are capable of maintaining running tabulations of a participant's benefits and payroll taxes, including half of benefits in adjusted gross income has been recommended for simplicity.[27]

Modifying the Indexation of Retirees' Benefits. Since 1975, when retirees' benefits were tied to percentage increases in the CPI, average covered earnings and the CPI have risen by about the same amount, and there have been several years when the CPI has risen faster. In those years when the CPI has increased more than wages, social security beneficiaries have been protected from inflation while real earnings of the average covered worker have declined. The true disparity between worker and recipient is even larger because workers must pay personal income and payroll taxes from earnings, whereas social security benefits are tax exempt. It is unreasonable that social security recipients fare better than workers who must support the program. It also seems clear that, if covered wages continue to rise less rapidly than prices, the current indexing scheme cannot be afforded.

It has been recommended that, on grounds of equity and financial soundness, retirees' benefits should be adjusted automatically to the lower of the rise in either wages, as measured by the percentage change in average hourly earnings (AHE), or prices. The average hourly earnings index may be preferred over an average wage index because it does not include fringe benefits and is adjusted for overtime. An alternative to the CPI for purposes of price indexation is the Personal Consumption Expenditure (PCE) chain index because it continually changes the market basket of goods and services that is priced to reflect changes in consumption patterns. (The CPI currently is based on a 1972–1973 market basket.) In addition, the PCE chain index measures housing costs by using a rental equivalence concept and thus avoids the volatility of changes in the CPI.[28]

An indexing procedure that switches between the lower of rises in wages and rises in prices would reduce real benefits if real wages declined. When productivity and real wages rise, as usually occurs, social security benefits would continue to be indexed by prices, and real benefits would be maintained. Estimating the financial impact of this indexation modification is difficult because the future pattern of wages and prices is unknown. As is shown in table 8, however, if the index switching procedure had been in place between 1975 and 1981, the cumulative OASDI cost saving would have been $27.3 billion if the lower of the increase in the AHE index and the increase in the PCE chain index had been used, or $21.0 billion if the lower of the increase in the AHE index and the increase in the CPI had been used. As a result, the combined OASDI trust fund ratio at the beginning of calendar 1982 would have been approximately 28 percent with the PCE chain index or 24 percent with the CPI, rather than 13 percent as anticipated by the 1981 trustees. Under such a switching proposal, unless real wages rise in each year, social security benefit increases would not keep pace with rises in the price index. The NCSS proposed a complicated recapture provision to increase real benefits when real wages rise after a period in which they have fallen.[29] Preferably, however, any benefit catch-up should be made ad hoc by Congress.

Another approach to protecting the system against persistently high inflation would be to place a cap on the automatic adjustment and allow

25

TABLE 8

ALTERNATIVE INDEXING PROCEDURES AND THE POTENTIAL SAVINGS FOR OASDI BENEFITS, 1975–1981

Calendar Year	Index (first quarter over first quarter percentage change)			OASDI Benefits (billions of dollars)	Savings from Lower of AHE Index[a] or	
	CPI	PCE chain	AHE[a]		CPI (billions of dollars)	PCE chain index (billions of dollars)
1975[b]	8.0	6.4	6.7	66.9	0.4	0.5
1976	6.4	5.8	7.2	75.7	0.9	1.2
1977	5.9	5.8	7.7	84.6	0.9	1.5
1978	6.5	6.1	7.8	92.9	1.0	1.8
1979	9.9	8.9	8.3	104.3	1.8	2.9
1980	14.3	10.4	8.4	121.3	6.1	7.3
1981[c]	11.2	10.0	9.9	137.3[d]	9.9	12.1
Total					21.0	27.3

[a] AHE is average hourly earnings.

[b] The index change in 1975 is calculated as the percentage change from 1974:2 to 1975:1 since ad hoc benefit increases were made through 1974:2.

[c] The savings in 1981 is much larger than would have occurred if the change in the indexing procedure had been instituted in 1981 because it captures the cumulative savings from previous years, particularly 1980, when real wages declined dramatically.

[d] Estimated by the Congressional Budget Office. It includes only benefit disbursements and not administrative costs or other program costs that are not indexed.

SOURCE: Computed by author and Robert Staiger of the Congressional Budget Office.

26

congressional review of the increase each year. This procedure is similar to the determination of federal civil service pay raises.[30]

Changing the indexing procedure would affect all OASDI recipients, regardless of their total income. Opponents of changes in the indexing procedure claim that recipients, particularly poor ones, could be hurt substantially, and many have no other means of keeping up with the rising cost of living. Instead, taxing a portion of benefits, discussed above, would avoid a large part of this problem because it would have no impact on recipients with low total income.

CONCLUDING COMMENTS

None of the proposals considered in this chapter would change the way the primary insurance amount is calculated. Social security student benefits, surviving benefits for parents of children sixteen and seventeen years old, the minimum benefit, and the lump-sum death benefit are all programs that are either excessive or redundant, or whose intent could be served better through modification of the SSI program. Phasing out the retirement test would increase benefits for the elderly who continue to remain active in the work force. The fact that those benefits would be disbursed to recipients whose total incomes are higher than the average recipient's provides added rationale for taxing benefits that exceed contributions. Taxing a portion of benefits would, however, have no impact on lower-income recipients who do not have income from other sources. Finally, modifying the indexation of benefits according to the switching proposal would reduce net benefits only if real wages decline. Besides its potential cost saving, this proposal would spread the burden of real wage declines between workers and recipients.

Excluding the indexing change, the combined cost-saving impact of these proposals would be $79.6 billion in fiscal years 1982–1986, roughly the same amount by which OASI outlays are projected to exceed OASI trust fund income. The cost saving would be even more if during any first-quarter-to-first-quarter period prices rise more rapidly than wages. (This is not anticipated after 1981, however, by the Reagan administration, the 1981 trustees' assumption paths I, II-A, or II-B, or the NCSS). If, in addition to these proposed changes, the increases in personal income taxes attributable to the taxation of benefits were reallocated into the OASI trust fund, the system would remain solvent. Although these proposals are usually discussed in the context of the short-run financing problem, their cost saving would accumulate over time and improve the system's long-run financial status. These changes, of course, would put nearly the entire financial burden of eliminating the short-run deficit on recipients rather than workers. This position could be tempered by phasing in the change in the tax treatment of benefits and increasing payroll taxes as needed.

27

Notes to Chapter 4

[1] U.S. Department of Health and Human Services, "Provisions of the Social Security Proposal," *HHS Fact Sheet,* May 12, 1981.

[2] National Commission on Social Security, *Social Security in America's Future,* March 1981, chapter 4.

[3] Dean Leimer, "Projected Rates of Return to Future Social Security Retirees under Alternative Benefit Structures," in Social Security Administration, Office of Research and Statistics, *Policy Analysis with Social Security Research Files: Proceedings of a Workshop Held March 1978 at Williamsburg, Virginia,* 1978.

[4] The EIC equals 10 percent of earned income up to $5,000 and is reduced for earnings or adjusted gross income between $6,000 and $10,000. For further detail on the EIC, see Colin D. Campbell and William L. Pierce, *The Earned Income Credit* (Washington, D.C.: American Enterprise Institute, 1980).

[5] This issue is discussed in more detail in Laurence J. Kotlikoff, "Social Security, Time to Reform," in Michael J. Boskin, ed., *Federal Tax Reform: Myths and Realities* (San Francisco: Institute for Contemporary Studies, 1978), pp. 119–45.

[6] See, for example, Russell Laxson, Donald MacNaughton, and David Rogers, "Dissenting Statement on Social Security Financing"; Robert Myers, "Dissenting Statement on Financing Social Security and Hospital Insurance from Other than Payroll Taxes"; and MacNaughton and Rogers, "Supplementary Statement on Financing Social Security Benefits from General Revenues," in NCSS, *Social Security in America's Future,* pp. 102–15.

[7] This approach has been recommended by the NCSS and is included in H.R. 3207, the social security financing bill proposed by Congressman J. J. Pickle (Democrat, Texas).

[8] Congressional Budget Office, *Paying for Social Security: Funding Options for the Near Term,* February 1981, p. 36.

[9] Ibid.

[10] The 1979 Advisory Council recommended reducing the taxable maximum so that the portion of covered wages that is taxable is the same as in 1979. See U.S. Department of Health, Education and Welfare, Advisory Council on Social Security, *Social Security Financing and Benefits,* December 1979, p. 2. In an attempt to reduce the ratio of taxable to covered wages without incurring an immediate decline in the growth of payroll taxes, the NCSS recommended holding the wage base in 1985 and 1986 at its 1984 level and then allowing it to resume its automatic increase. See NCSS, *Social Security in America's Future,* p. 22.

[11] The first major exception was the 1975 Advisory Council, which warned of ballooning costs and recommended several benefit cutbacks. See Secretary of

Health, Education and Welfare, *Reports of the Quadrennial Advisory Council on Social Security,* 1975. This issue is also discussed in Laxson, MacNaughton, and Rogers, "Dissenting Statement on Social Security Financing."

[12] One example is H.R. 3207, introduced by Congressman Pickle.

[13] Executive Office of the President, *Fiscal Year 1982 Budget Revisions,* March 1981, p. 127. If Reagan's social security reform package proposed in May 1981 were adopted, social security benefits would rise to 22.0 percent of total federal outlays by fiscal year 1986. See Executive Office of the President, *Mid-Session Review of the 1982 Budget,* July 15, 1981, p. 77.

[14] For a more detailed discussion of the profile of social security recipients and the distribution of benefits, see Mickey D. Levy, *The Tax Treatment of Social Security* (Washington, D.C.: American Enterprise Institute, 1980), chapter 2.

[15] Executive Office of the President, *America's New Beginning: A Program for Economic Recovery,* February 18, 1981, and *Fiscal Year 1982 Budget Revisions,* March 1981.

[16] U.S. Department of Health and Human Services, "Provisions of the Social Security Proposal."

[17] Appendix C summarizes the major social security financing proposals of the Reagan administration, H.R. 3207, the NCSS, the President's Commission on Pension Policy, and the 1979 Advisory Council.

[18] Social Security Administration, Office of the Actuary.

[19] In fiscal year 1981, federal outlays for student financial assistance and loan guarantees for students and parents, excluding Veterans Administration adjustment benefits (GI bill), will be approximately $5.9 billion.

[20] According to Sylvester Schieber, the windfall accruing to civil service retirees who also receive social security benefits would be reduced, but not eliminated, if the minimum benefit were abolished because of the highly graduated social security benefit structure. The Reagan administration recognizes this problem and has proposed a pension offset that would reduce social security benefits for beneficiaries who also receive pensions from federal civil service, state or local governments, or nonprofit organizations not covered by social security. See Sylvester Schieber, "Universal Social Security Coverage and Alternatives: Benefits and Costs" (Paper prepared for American Enterprise Institute Conference on Controlling the Cost of Social Security, June 25–26, 1981).

[21] Congressional Budget Office, *Reducing the Federal Budget: Strategies and Examples, Fiscal Years 1982–1986,* February 1981, p. 135.

[22] In each year after 1982, the level of excluded wages is indexed to percentage increases in average earnings.

[23] See Marshall Colberg, *The Social Security Retirement Test: Right or Wrong?* (Washington, D.C.: American Enterprise Institute, 1978).

[24] See, for example, NCSS, *Social Security in America's Future,* chapter 6.

[25] The administration's proposal did not include a provision to remove the exclusion of social security benefits from personal income taxes. The interaction between the retirement test and the tax treatment of benefits is discussed in Levy, *Tax Treatment of Social Security*, chapter 7.

[26] In 1978, recipients with total income (including social security) between $10,000 and $30,000 received approximately 30 percent of their total income from wages and proprietor's income. See Levy, *Tax Treatment of Social Security*, chapter 2.

[27] See, for example, the 1979 Advisory Council, *Social Security Financing and Benefits*.

[28] For an analysis of the differences between the CPI and the PCE index, see Robert J. Gordon, "The Consumer Price Index: Measuring Inflation and Causing It," *The Public Interest*, no. 63 (Spring 1981), pp. 112–34; and Phillip Cagan and Geoffrey H. Moore, *The Consumer Price Index: Issues and Alternatives* (Washington, D.C.: American Enterprise Institute, 1981).

[29] NCSS, *Social Security in America's Future*, chapter 7.

[30] This approach is discussed in Congressional Budget Office, *Paying for Social Security: Funding Options for the Near Term*, pp. 29–30.

5

THE LONG-RUN FINANCING ISSUE

According to the 1981 trustees' intermediate projections (paths II-A and II-B), OASDI expenditures as a percentage of taxable payroll will be about the same in 2010 as they are now. Because of assumed constant rises in real wages and the taxable maximum and a large increase in scheduled payroll tax rates in 1990, the OASI and DI trust funds will accumulate large balances for the next twenty-nine years. Then, in about 2010, the baby-boom children will begin to reach retirement age, and it is estimated that the ratio of workers to beneficiaries will begin to decline from its current level of three to one to less than two to one. As a consequence, OASI expenditures as a percentage of taxable payroll will rise rapidly, well beyond the 10.2 percent scheduled OASI payroll tax rate, and the OASI trust fund will plummet to unsafe, and then negative, levels. The accumulated balances in the DI trust fund, although large with respect to DI benefits, will not be sufficient to offset the financial decline of the OASI trust fund for any substantial period. In the 1981 trustees' projection path II-B, OASDI benefits exceed the scheduled OASDI payroll tax rate (12.4 percent) in every year after 2015. The funds are not expected to recover during the remainder of the seventy-five-year projection. Meanwhile, although the HI trust fund is projected to remain solvent in the short run, Medicare expenditures will rise rapidly in the 1980s, and the fund is expected to be exhausted under the 1981 trustees' projection path II-A in the early 1990s. The trust fund is not expected to recover through the remainder of the projection period. Table 9 displays the 1981 trustees' estimates of trust fund ratios for OASDI and HI under four projection paths: optimistic (path I), intermediate (paths II-A and II-B), and pessimistic (path III).

The gloomy long-run projections of social security are even more disturbing in light of their underlying assumptions. Under the 1981 trustees' intermediate projection path II-A, the long-run unemployment rate is 5 percent (after 1995), the long-run inflation rate is 3 percent (after 1990), the real wage differential is 2.00 percentage points (after 1995), and the long-run fertility rate is 2,100 births per 1,000 women. All of these key long-run assumptions are more optimistic than actual trends in the 1970s (see table 10), which in turn tended to be even more unfavorable than the "pessimistic" assumptions of official reports published in previous years.[1] Therefore, while I hope I am proved wrong by future events, I believe the 1981 trustees' assumptions for projection path II-A are too optimistic for assessing future

31

TABLE 9

1981 Trustees' Estimated Trust Fund Ratios of OASDI and Medicare (HI) Systems, Selected Calendar Years 1981–2055

Calendar Year	Optimistic Projection: Path I		Intermediate Projections: Path II-A		Path II-B		Pessimistic Projection: Path III	
	OASDI	HI	OASDI	HI	OASDI	HI	OASDI	HI
1981	18	46	18	46	18	46	18	46
1985	4	82	—1	70	—5	65	—	53
1990	45	106	20	51	—24	34	—	—
1995	166	63	100	—	—1	—	—	—
2000	321	n.a.	192	—	37	—	—	—
2005	496	—	290	—	91	—	—	—
2010	640	—	360	—	133	—	—	—
2015	705	—	370	—	132	—	—	—
2020	705	—	324	—	82	—	—	—
2025	672	—	240	—	—	—	—	—
2030	643	—	138	—	—	—	—	—
2035	636	—	29	—	—	—	—	—
2040	660	—	—	—	—	—	—	—
2045	702	—	—	—	—	—	—	—
2050	745	—	—	—	—	—	—	—
2055	786	—	—	—	—	—	—	—

NOTES: — indicates that the fund is projected to be exhausted and not to recover before the end of the projection period. n.a. = not available.

SOURCES: For OASDI, Board of Trustees, Federal Old-Age and Survivors Insurance and Disability Insurance Trust Funds, *1981 Annual Report*, 1981, p. 67; for HI, Board of Trustees, Federal Hospital Insurance Trust Fund, *1981 Annual Report*, 1981, p. 38.

realistic costs and benefits and are a poor basis for determining social security policy. The 1981 trustees' assumptions for projection path II-B are little better.

In addition, for simplification, the long-run assumptions do not include any economic fluctuations or variations in demographic factors (except for changes in real GNP growth rates to reflect the size and age-sex distribution of the population). This largely precludes interaction among the assumptions. It also assumes that economic and demographic trends are not sensitive to the rise in social security benefits and costs. Further, it presumes that trust fund balances absorb the year-to-year deficits incurred during brief economic downturns; the main text of the *1981 Annual Report* does not consider the impact of a sustained period of recession and inflation with several consecutive years of declining real wages, as occurred recently. Whether the assump-

TABLE 10

Selected Long-Run Economic and Demographic Assumptions Used in the 1981 Annual Report Compared with Actual Trends in the 1970s

Item	Long-Run Assumption Path[a]				Annual Average, 1970–1980
	Optimistic I	Intermediate II-A	II-B	Pessimistic III	
Real GNP (annual percent change)	3.5	3.1	2.7	2.2	3.2
Average covered wages (annual percent change)	4.5	5.0	5.5	6.0	7.2
CPI (average percent change)	2.0	3.0	4.0	5.0	7.8
Real wage differential (percentage points)	2.5	2.0	1.5	1.0	—0.6
Average annual interest rate (percent)[b]	5.1	5.6	6.1	6.6	7.3
Average annual unemployment rate (percent)	4.0	5.0	5.0	6.0	6.3
Total fertility rate[c]	2,400	2,100	2,100	1,700	1,917

[a] The long-run assumptions apply to the year 2000 and beyond for all items with the following exceptions: The annual percentage increase in real GNP is assumed to continue to change after the year 2000 to reflect the dependence of labor force growth on the size and age-sex distribution of the population. The percentage increases for the year 2055 are 3.4 for path I, 2.5 for path II-A, 2.1 for path II-B, and 0.9 for path III. In paths I, IIA, and II-B, the average real wage assumption applies to 1995 and beyond, and the inflation assumption applies to 1990 and beyond. The real wage differential applies to 1995 and beyond in all projections. The interest rate assumption applies to 1995 and beyond for path I and to 1990 and beyond under paths II-A and II-B. The unemployment rate assumption applies to 1995 and beyond under paths II-A and III.

[b] The average of interest rates determined in each of the twelve months of the year for special public-debt obligations issuable to the trust funds.

[c] The number of children who would be born to 1,000 women in their lifetimes if they were to experience the observed age-specific birthrates and were to survive the entire childbearing period.

Sources: *1981 Annual Report*, pp. 29, 32; and *Economic Report of the President*, January 1981.

tions are independent of themselves and also invariant to the growth of social security is a complex issue that should receive more attention in future efforts to conduct long-run projections.[2] The possible impact on economic growth is particularly important because of the expected expansion of social security. Appendix C of the trustees' *1981 Annual Report* analyzes the impact of economic cycles on operations of the trust funds. It projects fund balances based on several hypothesized economic cycles that fluctuate around its intermediate path II-B from 1981 to 1990. On the basis of their analysis, the trustees conclude that fluctuations of about 5 percent of trust fund ratios from their trend lines are likely to occur under normal economic cycles. Accordingly, minimum fund ratios should be 14 percent in order to accommodate normal economic cycles but, to be safe, a projected fund ratio below 20 percent "should be considered a clear call for action."[3]

The sensitivity of the amount of actuarial imbalance in the trust funds to the assumptions used is startling. (Actuarial imbalance is the average annual payroll rate minus OASDI expenditures as a percentage of taxable payroll.) As displayed in table 11, under the 1981 trustees' pessimistic projection path III, estimated average OASDI expenditures climb to nearly 28 percent of taxable payroll by the end of the projection period, as compared with 16 percent under path II-A and 17 percent under path II-B. During the period 2031–2055, the actuarial deficit would be 13.03 percent under path III, 3.39 percent under path II-A, and 4.41 percent under path II-B. The seventy-five-year average actuarial deficit also would be substantially larger under path III—6.25 percent of taxable payroll versus 0.93 percent under path II-A and 1.82 percent under path II-B.[4]

Medicare costs are projected to add substantially more to total social security expenditures and the combined actuarial imbalance, as shown in table 12. According to the 1981 trustees' projections, Medicare (HI) benefits will increase from 2.27 percent of taxable payroll in 1981 to 5.80 percent in 2005 and average 3.94 percent over the twenty-five-year period 1981–2005 under path II-A assumptions; they will climb to 6.38 percent of taxable payroll in 2005 and average 4.19 percent of taxable payroll under path II-B. These benefit levels are slightly higher than those projected in the 1980 trustees' intermediate projection. The HI trust fund would be exhausted in 1992 under projection path II-A, by 1991 under path II-B, and in 1989 under the pessimistic path III.

The trustees are only required to project HI benefits twenty-five years into the future. The Social Security Administration actuaries, however, provided for the NCSS seventy-five-year projections of HI benefits based on a blend of the economic projections of the Carter administration's 1980 midsession review and the 1980 trustees' intermediate assumptions through 2004 and the assumption that hospital costs will rise at the same rate as average covered wages thereafter.[5] Without the NCSS's cost-saving proposals, projections show HI expenditures as a percentage of taxable payroll climbing steadily and exceeding 8.4 percent in each year from 2030 to 2055, nearly three times the scheduled 2.9 percent HI tax rate. According to these projections, Medicare expenditures will exceed scheduled payroll taxes by an average of over 4 percent of taxable payroll over the seventy-five-year projection period. Table 12 shows the 1981 trustees' projections for paths II-A and II-B through 2005 and the NCSS's projections from 2010 through 2055. If hospital costs continue to grow faster than average covered wages, as they are expected to do during the next several decades, Medicare benefits would be substantially larger than these projections indicate.

34

If the economy performs according to the 1981 trustees' intermediate paths and if the NCSS's projections of Medicare costs are accurate, then combined OASDI plus Medicare benefits will reach approximately 25 percent of taxable payroll, or almost double current levels and scheduled payroll taxes, and the seventy-five-year actuarial deficit would exceed 5 percent of taxable payroll. However, under a blend of the path II-B and path III projections—a path that may be more realistic than path II-A—social security outlays would exceed 30 percent of taxable payroll, and the actuarial deficit would be even greater. If the assumptions of the pessimistic path III are realized, combined OASDHI benefits would approach 40 percent of taxable payroll.

The Conflict between Benefit Adequacy and Affordability

The clear lesson from these recent projections is that determination of the level of adequate benefits must be considered within the context of affordability. Traditional analyses of the role of social security have focused on the compromise between providing a fair rate of return to couples and one-earner families of all income classes based on their lifetime payroll contributions, on the one hand, and meeting the goal of social adequacy by providing needs-related benefits to the low-income elderly, on the other. The necessity of recognizing program affordability as the third dimension of concern may even intensify the conflict between the goals of individual equity and social adequacy by requiring the size and distribution of benefits to be justified not only in terms of the fair share to participants and the needs of certain recipients, but also in terms of the burdens placed on the economy as a whole and on the workers who must support the program.

In fiscal year 1981, under current law, OASDI benefits are expected to be $137.8 billion, or 21 percent of total federal budget outlays. By fiscal year 1986, the share of total federal outlays for OASDI benefits is expected to exceed 23 percent.[6] Total scheduled benefits will continue to grow as a percentage of the federal budget and economic output.

As real wages increase and individuals become wealthier (as implied by the long-run assumptions), average scheduled benefits per new retiree will rise, even after adjustment for inflation. According to projections based on the 1980 trustees' intermediate assumptions prepared by the Social Security Administration actuaries, real OASI benefits (measured in 1980 dollars) for a single worker with average wages retiring at age sixty-five will increase from $5,862 in 1980 to $10,500 in 2025 and to $17,322 in 2055. As shown in table 13, the real benefits of a single low-wage worker (someone who always earns the minimum wage) also will nearly triple, increasing from $3,859 in 1980 to $11,176 in 2055, while the inflation-adjusted benefits of a single high-wage earner (someone who always earns the taxable maximum) will be more than three and one-half times higher in 2055 than in 1980. Eligible married couples will receive benefits that are at least 50 percent higher.

35

TABLE 11

Estimated OASDI Expenditures, Taxes, and Actuarial Imbalance as a Percentage of Taxable Payroll under Alternative Projection Paths in the 1981 Annual Report, Selected Years 1981–2055

Calendar Year	Expenditures as a Percentage of Taxable Payroll[a]				Scheduled Tax Rate	Taxes Minus Expenditures as a Percentage of Taxable Payroll			
	I	II-A	II-B	III		I	II-A	II-B	III
1981	11.24	11.30	11.30	11.21	10.70	−0.54	−0.60	−0.60	−0.51
1985	10.85	11.10	11.63	12.04	11.40	0.55	0.30	−0.23	−0.64
1990	10.12	10.69	11.86	12.57	12.40	2.28	1.71	0.54	−0.17
1995	9.76	10.58	11.70	12.95	12.40	2.64	1.82	0.70	−0.55
2000	9.26	10.27	11.19	12.82	12.40	3.14	2.13	1.21	−0.42
2005	9.08	10.29	11.09	13.09	12.40	3.32	2.11	1.31	−0.69
2010	9.45	10.87	11.62	14.01	12.40	2.95	1.53	0.78	−1.61
2015	10.42	12.12	12.87	15.82	12.40	1.98	0.28	−0.47	−3.42
2020	11.56	13.64	14.43	18.17	12.40	0.84	−1.24	−2.03	−5.77

36

2025	12.52	15.05	15.92	20.70	12.40	−0.12	−2.65	−3.52	−8.30
2030	12.84	15.85	16.79	22.65	12.40	−0.44	−3.45	−4.39	−10.25
2035	12.63	16.04	17.03	23.98	12.40	−0.23	−3.64	−4.63	−11.58
2040	12.07	15.80	16.82	24.84	12.40	0.33	−3.40	−4.42	−12.44
2045	11.62	15.64	16.68	25.78	12.40	0.78	−3.24	−4.28	−13.38
2050	11.42	15.68	16.74	26.86	12.40	0.98	−3.28	−4.34	−14.46
2055	11.34	15.77	16.82	27.78	12.40	1.06	−3.37	−4.42	−15.38
25-year average									
1981–2005	9.99	10.67	11.51	12.55	11.94	1.95	1.27	0.43	−0.61
2006–2030	11.07	13.07	13.87	17.50	12.40	1.33	−0.67	−1.47	−5.10
2031–2055	11.92	15.79	16.81	25.43	12.40	0.48	−3.39	−4.41	−13.03
75-year average									
1981–2055	10.99	13.17	14.07	18.50	12.25	1.25	−0.93	−1.82	−6.25

a The economic and demographic assumptions underlying these four projection paths are summarized in table 10.

SOURCE: *1981 Annual Report*, pp. 63, 66.

TABLE 12

Medicare (HI) and Total OASDI plus Medicare Expenditures, Taxes, and Actuarial Imbalance as a Percentage of Taxable Payroll under Alternative Projection Paths in the 1981 Annual Report, Selected Years 1981–2055

	Medicare (HI)						OASDI plus Medicare (HI)					
	Expenditures as a percentage of taxable payroll[a]		Scheduled tax rate	Taxes minus expenditures as a percentage of taxable payroll		Expenditures as a percentage of taxable payroll[a]		Scheduled tax rate	Taxes minus expenditures as a percentage of taxable payroll	
Calendar Year	II-A	II-B		II-A	II-B		II-A	II-B		II-A	II-B
1981	2.27	2.27	2.60	0.33	0.33	13.57	13.57	13.3	−0.27	−0.27
1985	2.67	2.73	2.70	0.03	−0.03	13.77	14.36	14.1	0.33	−0.26
1990	3.39	3.55	2.90	−0.49	−0.65	14.08	15.41	15.3	1.22	−0.11
1995	4.27	4.55	2.90	−1.37	−1.65	14.85	16.25	15.3	0.45	−0.95
2000	5.04	5.44	2.90	−2.14	−2.54	15.31	16.63	15.3	−0.01	−1.33
2005	5.80	6.38	2.90	−2.90	−3.48	16.09	17.47	15.3	−0.79	−2.17
2010	5.78	5.78	2.90	−2.88	−2.88	16.65	17.40	15.3	−1.35	−2.10
2015	6.31	6.31	2.90	−3.41	−3.41	18.43	19.18	15.3	−3.13	−3.88

38

2020	7.01	7.01	2.90	−4.11	−4.11	20.65	21.44	15.3	−5.35	−6.14
2025	7.78	7.78	2.90	−4.88	−4.88	22.83	23.70	15.3	−7.53	−8.40
2030	8.42	8.42	2.90	−5.52	−5.52	24.27	25.21	15.3	−8.97	−9.91
2035	8.72	8.72	2.90	−5.82	−5.82	24.76	25.75	15.3	−9.46	−10.45
2040	8.77	8.77	2.90	−5.87	−5.87	24.57	25.59	15.3	−9.27	−10.29
2045	8.69	8.69	2.90	−5.79	−5.79	24.33	25.37	15.3	−9.03	−10.07
2050	8.64	8.64	2.90	−5.74	−5.74	24.32	25.38	15.3	−9.02	−10.08
2055	8.63	8.63	2.90	−5.73	−5.73	24.40	25.45	15.3	−9.10	−10.15
25-year average										
1981–2005	3.94	4.19	2.81	−1.13	−1.38	14.61	15.70	14.75	0.14	−0.95
2006–2030	6.80[b]	6.80[b]	2.90	−3.90[b]	−3.90[b]	19.87	20.67	15.3	−4.57	−5.37
2031–2055	8.69[b]	8.69[b]	2.90	−5.79[b]	−5.79[b]	24.48	25.50	15.3	−9.18	−10.20
75-year average										
1981–2055	7.00[b]	7.08[b]	2.88	−4.12[b]	−4.20[b]	20.17	21.15	15.13	−5.04	−6.02

[a] Expenditure estimates for HI beyond 2005 are based on the NCSS economic assumptions, which assume that hospital costs rise at the same rate as average covered wages.

[b] Estimated by author.

SOURCES: For OASDI expenditures for all years and Medicare (HI) expenditures through 2005, *1981 Annual Report*, pp. 63, 66, and *1981 Annual Report* of the HI trust fund, p. 35; for Medicare expenditures after 2005, Social Security Administration, Office of the Actuary.

TABLE 13
REAL SCHEDULED OASI BENEFITS FOR A SINGLE WORKER RETIRING AT AGE SIXTY-FIVE, SELECTED YEARS 1980–2055
(in 1980 dollars)

Calendar Year	Low-Wage Worker[a]	Average-Wage Worker	High-Wage Worker[b]
1980	3,859	5,862	7,437
1985	3,494	5,245	6,803
1990	3,735	5,632	7,513
1995	4,084	6,169	8,436
2000	4,506	6,820	9,666
2005	4,925	7,503	11,018
2010	5,325	8,176	12,357
2015	5,744	8,887	13,681
2020	6,243	9,660	14,963
2025	6,775	10,500	16,334
2030	7,364	11,414	17,809
2035	8,005	12,407	19,395
2040	8,702	13,486	21,092
2045	9,459	14,660	22,929
2050	10,281	15,935	24,925
2055	11,176	17,322	27,095

NOTE: These estimates are based on the 1980 trustees' intermediate projections, which assume a long-run real wage differential of 1.75 percentage points. The growth of real benefits would be smaller with a lower real wage differential.

[a] A low-wage worker is someone who always earns the minimum wage.

[b] A high-wage worker is someone who always earns the taxable maximum under social security.

SOURCE: Social Security Administration, Office of the Actuary, unpublished memo.

Whether the goal of social security adequacy requires that real scheduled benefits increase as fast as the growth in real wages is brought into question by the issue of affordability. Another related issue concerning the role of social security is whether scheduled real benefits should continue to grow when the government is now seriously considering policies that would increase the rate of personal saving. In addition, even if scheduled benefits are not modified, it is questionable whether the trust fund balances should be allowed to increase so tremendously before the period when the baby-boom children reach retirement age, or whether payroll tax rates should be trimmed. In the year 2010, for example, under projection path II-A, OASDI trust fund balances will exceed 30 percent of taxable payroll.

An oversimplified calculation can illustrate the scheduled growth of the program: imposing on the current federal budget 18.5 percent of taxable wages—the level of OASDI benefits in the year 2025 under a blend of the path II-B and path III projections—rather than the current benefit level of 11.2 percent would add $86.8 billion to fiscal year 1981 federal outlays.[7] This increase excludes the impact of higher Medicare benefits. Such an increase could not be afforded unless real wages grow as fast as the projections assume.

Whether these levels of projected benefits are sustainable depends on the magnitude of competing demands for government spending, the willingness of wage earners and proprietors to continue to support the program, and the impact of these expanding taxes on economic growth. The experience of other industrialized countries does not provide conclusive answers about the future affordability of social security. Although many countries provide higher social insurance benefits that require higher payroll tax contributions than in the United States, their defense expenditures, as a percentage of either total government spending or GNP, are much lower.[8] In addition, many of their social insurance programs currently are facing large financial difficulties, and their benefits may be trimmed.[9]

My general but untestable observation is that for the United States to provide social security and Medicare benefits significantly larger than estimated by the intermediate projections would be difficult to sustain over a lengthy period, unless the demand for other government goods and services, such as defense, declines unexpectedly. Higher benefits could be afforded if today's young workers follow the example of their parents and reproduce sufficiently high numbers of offspring who would enter the work force in the next twenty to thirty years, offset the expected decline in the worker-to-dependent ratio, and reduce benefits as a percentage of taxable payroll. Even though the birthrate has increased slightly since the mid-1970s, it should not be expected to climb by roughly 50 percent from its trough and match the average birthrate of the 1950s. In addition, mortality rates are expected to continue to decline, leading to higher average lifetime benefits for longer-lived beneficiaries and to lower worker-to-dependent ratios. Higher than expected economic growth similarly would make the scheduled benefits more affordable; but this pattern should not be counted on.

ACHIEVING LONG-RUN TRUST FUND SOLVENCY

Even if projected future benefits were sustainable, their ballooning size raises the issue of the growing financial conflict between workers who must incur higher tax burdens to support rising real benefits and the persons who receive them. As Colin Campbell states, "The future stability of the social security system may depend on the way in which Congress decides to distribute the increasing cost of the system between taxpayers and beneficiaries."[10] Holding scheduled benefits constant and allowing payroll taxes to adjust upward places the entire burden of future increases on workers. In effect, this approach

41

would continually test the willingness of workers to pay taxes to support the program. The increasing political power of recipients relative to the non-recipients might lead to intense intergenerational conflict and abrupt policy changes, particularly if the higher benefits were found to have undesirable consequences on economic growth. In contrast, the entire burden can be placed on recipients by holding payroll tax rates constant and adjusting scheduled benefits to reflect the ratio of dependents to workers, among other items.[11] This, of course, would substantially reduce the average expected real rates of return for today's younger workers (or may spark another baby boom) and is not politically feasible.

A middle ground is to trim benefits and partially mitigate required hikes in taxes. Besides the possible benefit cuts described in the short-run financing section, several other changes with primarily long-run impacts are discussed below. Each could be phased in over a period of time so that retirees or persons soon to retire would not be affected.

Universal Social Security Coverage. Although extending social security coverage to all wages earned by government employees is usually supported for equity reasons, it would also have a large beneficial effect on social security financing.[12] The NCSS estimates that extending coverage to all new federal, state, and local government employees would save an average of 0.55 percent of taxable payroll averaged over the next seventy-five years. This accounts for more than half the estimated average actuarial imbalance of the OASDI programs in the 1981 trustees' projection path II-A and about a third of the actuarial imbalance in path II-B. A sizable portion of the financial saving from universal coverage is attributable to the elimination of the windfall benefits that go to retired government employees who receive both government retirement benefits and social security benefits. Therefore, the financial savings of universal coverage would be less if it were implemented after elimination of the windfall benefits. Extending coverage would increase future payroll taxes more than benefits because of above-average government wages coupled with the highly graduated benefit structure. In addition, extending coverage to the remaining (uncovered) earnings of dual beneficiaries would involve smaller benefit obligations for the social security fund than "first-dollar coverage" (since they already receive at least the social security minimum benefit), while payroll taxes by these individuals would remain proportional to earnings up to the taxable maximum.

Allowing government employment to remain uncovered by social security cannot be justified. The goal of universal coverage should be adopted immediately regardless of the financial status of the social security program.[13] That goal receives even stronger support since the exclusion is a great financial drain on the system. Of course, the primary objection to extending coverage to federal government employees comes from the civil servants themselves, who will receive civil service retirement benefits that are far more generous than those they could expect under social security. In addition, some people object to universal coverage simply because it would expand a program they would rather reduce in scope (preferably, they would make social security participation voluntary). This opposition is based on a goal that is not within the range of politically feasible policy alternatives and should be regarded with skepticism.[14]

The Retirement Age. Increasing the age at which full retirement benefits would be available from sixty-five to sixty-eight has been recommended recently by the 1979 Advisory Council, the NCSS, the President's Commission on Pension Policy, and Congressman J. J. Pickle (H.R. 3207) for several reasons. First, since 1935, when the retirement age was arbitrarily set at sixty-five, Americans have tended to live longer, and their life expectancy is expected to rise even higher. The actuaries of the Social Security Administration estimate that life expectancy for men sixty-five years old in the year 2000 will be nearly three and one-half years higher than in 1940; for women, seven and one-half years.[15] In addition, older people probably are healthier today than in earlier years, and the impact of poor health on their potential work has declined.[16]

Second, higher social security wealth, the Social Security Amendments of 1961, which allowed men to retire at age sixty-two with actuarially reduced benefits, the retirement test, and the expansion of DI benefits have all been identified as factors underlying the trend toward early retirement.[17] Labor force participation rates of older men have declined rapidly: from 81.2 percent in 1960 to 61.8 percent in 1979 for men aged sixty to sixty-four and from 46.8 percent in 1960 to 29.6 percent in 1979 for men aged sixty-five to sixty-nine.[18] The trend toward early retirement has reduced taxable earnings and sped up social security benefit disbursements. In addition, it has reduced the nation's productive capacity, which may have an adverse impact on the long-run financing issue.

Third, increasing the retirement age would partially offset the reduction in the ratio of workers to beneficiaries when the baby-boom children retire. The NCSS estimates that gradually increasing the retirement age from sixty-five to sixty-eight over the period 2000–2012 would reduce benefits by 1.07 percent of taxable payroll averaged over the seventy-five-year projection period 1981–2055. This would erase the entire actuarial imbalance for OASDI estimated under the 1981 trustees' path II-A and three-fifths of the imbalance under path II-B. The savings would be even larger if the change were implemented earlier.

Some opponents of increasing the retirement age argue that many people must retire before the age of sixty-five because of poor health, and increasing the retirement age would not be fair.[19] Although poor health has been identified as one factor that forces workers to retire early, the health of the elderly has improved, and it has not been a factor that has added to the trend toward early retirement.[20]

Others, including the Reagan administration, would keep sixty-five as the age of "normal retirement," but would tilt the benefit adjustment factors so as to reduce benefits to early retirees and thereby provide financial encouragement to delay retirement. The current benefit adjustment factors, under Social Security Administration assumptions, yield benefits for persons retiring between ages sixty-two and sixty-five that are actuarially equivalent to those for a person retiring at age sixty-five, whereas benefits for persons retiring after age sixty-five are below the equivalent level.[21]

The Reagan administration proposal would reduce benefits for early retirees so that persons retiring at sixty-two would receive 55 percent of the benefits they would receive if they postponed retirement until sixty-five; currently they receive 80 percent. This reduction in benefits for early retirees would encourage higher labor force participation by persons sixty-two to sixty-five, but would still provide benefits to persons who choose to take early retirement because of poor health or any other reason. According to the Reagan administration, this modification of the benefit adjustment factors and its expected impact on later retirement would save 1.30 percent of taxable payroll averaged throughout the seventy-five-year projection period.[22]

Congress opposes the Reagan administration proposal in part because it would be effective beginning in January 1982. Benefit cuts of this magnitude should be phased in over several years so that older workers can adjust their plans in light of the new policy. Congressional debate on this issue is likely. Also, modifying the benefit adjustment factors may be a complement to or a substitute for raising the retirement age. Congressman Pickle's H.R. 3207, for example, would gradually increase the normal retirement age to sixty-eight but would modify the benefit adjustment factors so that workers could retire with reduced benefits any time after age sixty-two.

The Benefit Formula and the Calculation of Earnings Histories and the "Bend Points." The 1977 amendments corrected a flaw in the procedure for calculating the PIA—albeit with an unnecessarily long transition period—by indexing both earnings histories and the benefit brackets, or "bend points," to percentage changes in average wages and by keeping the marginal benefit rates constant. The provision for indexing benefits by the CPI was not changed.

The Reagan administration has proposed modifying the procedure in the years 1982–1987 by indexing the bend points by one-half of the increase in average wages for those attaining age sixty-two (or dying or becoming disabled), while continuing to index the earnings record used to compute the average indexed monthly earnings by the full percentage increase in average covered wages. The full adjustment of the bend points would occur in each year after 1987. The Reagan administration states that this temporary change would reduce benefits for calendar years 1982–1986 by $17.6 billion under the economic assumptions in the president's March 1981 budget revisions and by an average of 1.30 percent of taxable payroll over the next seventy-five years.[23]

The issue of indexation and how to calculate the PIA has been analyzed in detail elsewhere; so this section will focus primarily on the costs of alternative procedures and their basic differences.[24] However, because the procedure for indexing earnings histories and the bend points is often misunderstood—despite its large impact on the goals of individual equity, social adequacy, and program affordability—a word of caution is appropriate. The indexing procedure is only one facet of the basic benefit formula.[25] It should not be changed for the sole purpose of slowing the growth of future benefits if the change has undesirable effects on program equity and if other ways are available to slow the growth of benefits without unwanted side effects.[26] The desired level and distribution of social security benefits may be altered by changing the procedure for calculating earnings histories and the bend points, by changing the benefit formula's marginal benefit rates, or in several other ways. Therefore, changes in the current indexing procedure should be considered with caution and evaluated against more straightforward modifications of the benefit formula that may involve fewer complications or unintended consequences.

Indexing each worker's prior earnings and the benefit formula's bend points to changes in average wages has been supported because over time it maintains constant average "replacement ratios"—the ratio of initial benefits to earnings the year before retirement—and thereby provides generous increases in real benefits as real wages rise. One argument against the wage-indexing scheme is that, as individuals become wealthier (as is assumed in the long-run projections), it is questionable whether the scope of social security should be expanded to provide the large rises in real benefits that would occur under wage indexing.

This general issue of what level of benefits is adequate should depend ultimately on the level considered affordable and not on the average replacement ratio, which is a highly misleading measure for evaluating social security policy. The replacement ratio is based on earnings the year before retirement, rather than on a worker's lifetime earnings; thus, it does not reflect a worker's lifetime payroll taxes and does not measure rates of return on those contributions. It is also misleading because a declining average replacement ratio is often interpreted as a decline in real benefits, which is not necessarily the case. Finally, benefits are exempt from all forms of taxation, while earnings in the year before retirement (the denominator in the ratio) are subject to income and payroll taxation.

William C. Hsiao and several other experts have recommended indexing average monthly earnings and the bend points to inflation rather than to increases in average covered wages.[27] This procedure would allow real benefits to increase in future years, but at a slower rate than under the wage-indexing

TABLE 14

Real Benefits and Replacement Rates for Single Average-Wage Earners under Current Law and Alternative Benefit Schedules, Selected Years 1980–2055

Year	Index AIME and Bend Points by Wages (Current Law)		Index AIME and Bend Points by CPI after 2000		Index AIME by Wages and Bend Points by CPI after 2000	
	Benefit (1980 dollars)	Replacement rate[a] (percent)	Benefit (1980 dollars)	Replacement rate[a] (percent)	Benefit (1980 dollars)	Replacement rate[a] (percent)
1980	5,862	51.1	5,862	51.1	5,862	51.1
1985	5,245	42.5	5,245	42.5	5,245	42.5
1990	5,632	41.7	5,632	41.7	5,632	41.7
1995	6,169	41.4	6,169	41.4	6,169	41.4

Year						
2000	6,820	41.5	6,820	41.5	6,820	41.5
2005	7,503	41.7	7,184	39.9	7,398	41.1
2010	8,176	41.8	7,340	37.5	7,888	40.3
2015	8,887	41.8	7,551	35.5	8,396	39.5
2020	9,660	41.8	7,844	33.9	8,839	38.2
2025	10,500	41.8	8,225	32.7	9,121	36.3
2030	11,414	41.8	8,700	31.8	9,427	34.5
2035	12,407	41.8	8,989	30.3	9,763	32.9
2040	13,486	41.8	9,286	28.7	10,125	31.4
2045	14,660	41.8	9,607	27.4	10,520	30.0
2050	15,935	41.8	9,957	26.1	10,949	28.7
2055	17,322	41.8	10,336	24.9	11,415	27.5

NOTE: These estimates are based on the 1980 trustees' intermediate projections, which assume a long-run real wage differential of 1.75 percentage points. With slower growth in real wages, the growth of real benefits would be slower, and the alternative benefit schedules would have a smaller impact on real benefits and replacement rates than indicated in this table.

[a] The replacement rate is the ratio of initial benefits to earnings the year before retirement.

SOURCE: Social Security Administration, Office of the Actuary, unpublished memo.

47

scheme (see table 14). If both the AIME and the bend points were indexed to the CPI beginning in the year 2000, inflation-adjusted benefits would grow more slowly than under the wage-indexed scheme, and replacement ratios would decline with increases in real wages as workers are pushed into higher brackets in the graduated benefit formula. For the single average-wage earner, however, the ratio of initial benefits to earnings in the year before retirement would decline to 30.3 percent in 2035—a replacement ratio similar to the average rate existing in 1969 before the generous benefit increases of the early 1970s.[28] If only the bend points were indexed to inflation beginning in 2000, while the current procedure for calculating earnings histories was left intact, the growth in real benefits would be slower than under current law but somewhat faster than under the Hsiao proposal. Although this is an arbitrary approach to changing the calculation of benefits, it is included because some of the architects of the Reagan administration reform proposal considered it.

The Reagan administration proposal to limit the increase in the bend points to one-half of the increase in average covered wages in 1982–1987 would push recipients into higher benefit brackets faster than under the Hsiao proposal. Its temporary nature, however, would limit its long-run cost-saving ability and, even with its passage, the threat of long-run insolvency would remain.

CONCLUDING COMMENTS

The majority of recent reports on social security by the trustees of the system and other official bodies have tended to underestimate the program's short-run financial problems and, although they project long-run actuarial imbalances, in general they imply that there is no immediate need to address the issue of long-run insolvency. The 1979 Advisory Council on Social Security, for example, projected substantial increases in program benefits as a percentage of taxable payroll, but concluded that "the costs of social security will not become an intolerable burden on taxpayers in future years" and, in the event adverse demographic and economic trends continue, "there is more than enough time and there are several ways to deal with them."[29] In this respect, such reports have reinforced the tendency of Congress to delay making decisions before crises occur. In addition, the reports tend to suggest that the short-run financial problem can be solved largely by reallocating funds. Unfortunately, such an approach would delay necessary reform.

On the other hand, the tenor of the *1981 Annual Report,* if not its projections, reflects the seriousness of the financing problem, and the Reagan administration has proposed a financing reform package that includes numerous cuts in benefits. In addition, the 1979 Advisory Council, the NCSS, and the President's Commission on Pension Policy have recommended reductions in several benefit programs, and at least one has recommended relatively major changes, such as raising the retirement age, taxing a portion of benefits, making coverage universal, and changing the procedure for indexing benefits. Combined, the recommendations of these reports and of the Reagan administration provide Congress with a wide range of social security reform proposals. Of course, the portion of the long-run actuarial deficit eliminated by a reform package depends on future demographic and economic trends. Also, the problem of growing Medicare costs remains, and it was not addressed in the administration's reform package.

Although anticipating long-run economic and demographic trends is virtually impossible, the intermediate assumptions used by the 1980 and 1981 trustees and the NCSS seem too optimistic. Accordingly, social security benefits will probably rise higher and actuarial deficits be larger than levels indicated by the intermediate projections. In response, selected cuts of non-earnings-related benefits and a change in the procedure for indexing benefits should be implemented immediately. The cost savings from these changes would accumulate over time. In addition, Congress should begin now to tackle several long-run issues that would require lengthy implementation periods: the benefit adjustment factors and the retirement age; the calculation of the PIA and the indexation of earnings histories and the benefit formula's bend points; and universal coverage. If Congress decides now to alter the age-related benefit adjustment factors or to increase the retirement age during some future period, it could reverse that decision if the financial outlook of social security improved. Although Congress should seriously consider changing the procedure for indexing earnings histories and benefit brackets, any such change should be evaluated in terms of individual equity and social adequacy and not just its impact on long-run program costs. Finally, the goal of universal coverage should be adopted immediately regardless of the financial status of the social security program.

As this study has indicated, Congress may attempt to resolve the short-run financing problem by reallocating funds or financing from the general fund, by increasing payroll taxes, or by trimming benefits. Reallocating funds would not improve the financial soundness of the system; it would only delay necessary reform and shift the mounting political burden imposed by the program from the current Congress onto future Congresses. The traditional approach of relying fully on payroll tax increases to avoid the short-run financial imbalance would be more straightforward and would better reflect the true costs of the program, but it would similarly sidestep the issue of affordability of future scheduled benefits. Trimming benefits would be consistent with other budget-cutting measures pending in Congress and would represent a responsible step toward ensuring the program's long-run financial soundness.

NOTES TO CHAPTER 5

[1] For an in-depth comparison of projections in previous annual reports, see Colin Campbell, "The Exploding Cost of Social Security," in William Fellner, project director, *Contemporary Economic Problems: Demand, Productivity, and Population* (Washington, D.C.: American Enterprise Institute, 1981).

[2] This issue is addressed in the "Report of the Panel of Consultants to the 1979 Advisory Council on Social Security," in U.S. Department of Health, Education and Welfare, Advisory Council on Social Security, *Social Security Financing and Benefits,* December 1979, appendix B, pp. 255–362.

[3] Board of Trustees, Federal Old-Age and Survivors Insurance, Disability Insurance, and Hospital Insurance Trust Funds, *1981 Annual Report,* 1981, appendix C, p. 98. The impact of social security financing on economic cycles is also analyzed in U.S. Congress, House of Representatives, Subcommittee on Social Security of the Committee on Ways and Means, *Social Security and Economic Cycles,* 96th Congress, 2d session, November 1980. The study concludes: "Since future cycles in the national economy are to be expected, this analysis points to the need for social security financing planning which involves accumulation and maintenance of adequate reserves" (p. 2).

[4] For a given real wage differential, a higher rate of inflation provides a higher level of social security benefits as a percentage or taxable payroll, but a lower actuarial deficit. This occurs because a worker's earnings history is indexed to average wages only through age sixty.

The actuarial deficits projected by the 1980 trustees were slightly larger than those projected by the 1981 trustees. The 1980 trustees' intermediate assumptions were almost the same as the 1981 trustees' path II-B (except that they assumed a 1.75-percentage-point real wage differential and 2.8 percent annual growth of real GNP), and their projections did not include the Reagan administration's cost-saving proposals. Thus, in the 1980 trustees' intermediate projections, OASDI benefits grew to over 17 percent of taxable payroll, and the average annual actuarial deficit over the seventy-five-year projection period was 1.52 percent of taxable payroll. The 1980 trustees' pessimistic path was also based on more pessimistic assumptions than the 1981 trustees' path III (it assumed a total fertility rate of 1,500 births per 1,000 women and an average inflation rate of 6.0 percent, but a more optimistic real wage differential of 1.25 percentage points). As a consequence, it projected OASDI benefits to grow to nearly 30 percent of taxable payroll, but an average annual actuarial deficit over the seventy-five-year projection period of 6.17 percent of taxable payroll.

[5] National Commission on Social Security, *Social Security in America's Future,* March 1981, chapter 4.

[6] This is true under both the Carter and the Reagan versions of the budget for fiscal year 1982.

[7] The Social Security Administration actuaries estimate that total taxable wages in fiscal year 1981 will be $1,188.7 billion.

[8] For example, in Austria, the Netherlands, and Sweden, where 1981 payroll tax rates for OASDI range from 21 percent to 35 percent (and payroll tax rates for all social insurance programs range from 35 to 58 percent), defense expenditures range from 4 to 12 percent of total central government spending. In comparison, in the United States in 1981, defense expenditures will constitute approximately 24 percent of total outlays. Under the Reagan administration budget, they are projected to exceed 37 percent of total federal outlays in 1986.

[9] Many industrial countries have recognized a financing dilemma and have taken steps to slow the growth of future benefit increases. For example, several countries (including Italy, Belgium, West Germany, and Finland) have placed a cap on indexing of benefits or have otherwise altered the indexing procedure. Also, several countries that have hitherto exempted social security benefits from personal income taxes have taken steps to change this policy. See Joseph G. Simanis, "Worldwide Trends in Social Security, 1979," *Social Security Bulletin,* vol. 43, no. 8 (August 1980), pp. 6–9; and A. Delperee, "Social Security Cash Benefits in a Period of Concurrent Inflation and Recession," in *Problems in Social Security under Economic Recession and Inflation* (Geneva: International Social Security Association, 1978), pp. 13–24.

[10] Campbell, "The Exploding Cost of Social Security," p. 307.

[11] This approach and others were analyzed in Richard A. Musgrave, "Financing Social Security: A Reappraisal," Discussion Paper no. 753 (Cambridge, Mass.: Harvard University, Harvard Institute of Economic Research, April 1980).

[12] See Department of Health, Education and Welfare, Universal Social Security Coverage Group, *The Desirability and Feasibility of Social Security Coverage to Employees of Federal, State, and Local Governments and Nonprofit Organizations,* March 1980; NCSS, *Social Security in America's Future,* chapter 8; Mickey D. Levy, "The Case for Extending Social Security Coverage to Government Employees," *Journal of Risk and Insurance,* vol. 47, no. 1 (March 1980), pp. 78–90; and Sylvester Schieber, "Universal Social Security Coverage and Alternatives: Benefits and Costs" (Paper prepared for American Enterprise Institute Conference on Controlling the Cost of Social Security, June 25–26, 1981).

[13] Extending coverage to all state and local government employees involves a different set of implementation problems—both economic and legal—and should be considered separately from extending coverage to federal government employees. Extending coverage only to new government employees would allow the current inequities and financial drain to last for about forty years. A more rapid transition could involve immediate coverage of all government employees, with benefits based on a weighted average of projected rates of return on contributions to the different pensions (see Levy, "The Case for Extending Social Security Coverage to Government Employees," appendix). In either case, government pensions would be modified to supplement social security, analogous to corporate pensions.

51

[14] The Reagan administration's social security package did not include a provision to extend coverage to government wages.

[15] NCSS, *Social Security in America's Future*, p. 124.

[16] Ibid., pp. 124–27.

[17] See Robert L. Clark and David T. Barker, *Reversing the Trend toward Early Retirement* (Washington, D.C.: American Enterprise Institute, 1981), chapter 3. One fact that reveals the large effect of allowing retirement at the age of sixty-two is that before 1961 labor force participation rates of men declined continuously with age, with the greatest percentage-point drop occurring between the ages of sixty-four and sixty-five; in the 1970s, there have been two large prominent percentage-point drops in participation rates, occurring between the ages of sixty-one and sixty-two and between sixty-four and sixty-five.

[18] NCSS, *Social Security in America's Future*, p. 129.

[19] For example, see Wilbur Cohen, Elizabeth Duskin, and Joyce Miller, "Dissenting Statement on Raising the Retirement Age," in NCSS, *Social Security in America's Future*, pp. 330–34.

[20] Clark and Barker, *Reversing the Trend toward Early Retirement*, chapter 3.

[21] Specifically, benefits are reduced by five-ninths of one percent for each month between the retirement age and sixty-five, whereas persons who postpone receiving benefits past sixty-five have benefits increased by one-twelfth of one percent a month (for persons attaining the age of sixty-five in 1982 and after, this fraction will be increased to one-fourth of one percent). A person who starts receiving benefits at sixty-two will receive monthly 80 percent of the amount that he would receive if he had postponed retirement until sixty-five.

[22] U.S. Department of Health and Human Services, "Provisions of the Social Security Proposal," May 12, 1981, p. 6.

[23] Ibid. As is discussed in appendix A, the cost saving from this proposal may be less because new recipients have the option through 1983 of receiving benefits based on the old benefit formula.

[24] See, for example, William C. Hsiao, "An Optimal Indexing Method for Social Security"; Lawrence H. Thompson, "Indexing Social Security: The Options"; and Robert S. Kaplan, "A Comparison of Rates of Return to Social Security Retirees under Wage and Price Indexing," in Colin D. Campbell, ed., *Financing Social Security* (Washington, D.C.: American Enterprise Institute, 1978), pp. 19–90, 119–44.

[25] The new social security benefit formula is described in appendix A.

[26] Specification of the AIME determines which workers should receive the same benefit award and which should receive smaller or larger amounts. Analogously, the definition of taxable income implicitly determines "who the equals are" for assessing personal income tax liability. Like the level of social security benefits, personal income tax receipts may be altered by changing the width of the personal

income tax brackets or the marginal tax rates, rather than by respecifying taxable income. Achieving equity, however, is even more difficult in social security than in personal income taxes because of its intertemporal nature. See Dean R. Leimer, Ronald Hoffman, and Alan Freiden, "A Framework for Analyzing the Equity of the Social Security Benefit Structure," Social Security Administration, Office of Research and Statistics, *Studies in Income Distribution,* no. 6, January 1978.

[27] See, for example, Hsiao, "An Optimal Indexing Method for Social Security," and Kaplan, "A Comparison of Rates of Return to Social Security Retirees under Wage and Price Indexing."

[28] In 1969, the replacement rate based on a single worker with an average earnings history was 30.8 percent. Legislated rises in benefits in the following three years increased the replacement rate to 42.3 percent in 1975 and 51.1 percent in 1980. When the benefit formula established by the 1977 amendments is fully implemented, the average rate will level off at about 41 percent.

[29] Advisory Council on Social Security, *Social Security Financing and Benefits,* 1979, pp. 26, 47.

Appendix A

The Social Security Benefit Formula Established by the 1977 Amendments

Social security retirement benefits are based on the primary insurance amount (PIA), adjusted for early or delayed retirement and the family characteristics of the recipient (the PIA is the basis for determining dependents' and survivors' benefits). The total benefit amount is adjusted upward each June in proportion to increases in the CPI.

The PIA is determined by first calculating each worker's average monthly earnings and then applying the benefit formula's marginal benefit rates to the average monthly earnings. The Social Security Amendments of 1977 established that a worker's annual wages be indexed to the average wages of all workers before they are converted into average monthly earnings. This is done by multiplying each preceding year's wage by the ratio of the average wage of all workers two years before the year in which a worker reaches the age of sixty-two to the average wage in the year the wage is earned. The resulting average indexed monthly earnings (AIME) form the benefit base in the benefit formula.

The benefit base is divided into three brackets, as shown below. The three bend points that determine the width of the benefit brackets are indexed to average wages. Since both earnings histories of workers and the bend points of the benefit base are indexed to increases in average wages, a mythical worker earning the average wage in each year and retiring in the future will have the same portion of earnings in each benefit bracket as does an "average wage earner" retiring in 1984.[1]

New Social Security Benefit Formula in 1981		
Average Indexed Monthly Earnings (dollars)	*Marginal Benefit Rate (percent)*	*Primary Insurance Amount (dollars)*
First $211	90	189.90
Next $1,063	32	340.16
Remainder above $1,274	15	

The marginal benefit rates that are applied to the AIME in each bracket are steeply graduated, providing the highest benefit per dollar of AIME to low-income earners. The marginal benefit rates remain constant from year to year. The PIA is the sum of the marginal benefit rates multiplied by the AIME in each benefit bracket. In 1981, for example, under the new benefit formula the PIA of an individual with an AIME of $950 would be $426 (90 percent of $211 plus 32 percent of $739). Since an individual's AIME does not change after retirement and the formula's marginal benefit rates remain constant, a person's benefit amount changes only with increases in the CPI, unless his family characteristics change.

Although the 1977 amendments corrected the long-run financing problem attributable to the indexing flaw, they provided a very long transition period that allows persons who retire before 1984 to receive benefits more generous than intended at a large cost to the system. The amendments included a "transition guarantee" under which any person retiring before January 1, 1984, could choose between benefits calculated under the new formula and those yielded by a calculation that involved the old formula.[2] Retirees initially electing the old formula calculation could subsequently shift to the new formula at any time before 1984.

It was originally expected that as the transition period progressed, an increasing number of retirees would elect to use the new formula, and that would have happened if there had been growth in average real wages. But because of recent declines in real wages, use of the old formula calculation continues to yield higher benefits for a large portion of new retirees. These retirees, in effect, are permitted to profit from the overindexing that occurred between 1972 and 1978 and receive substantially larger benefits than new retirees in 1984. In addition, the advantage to many of those who reach the eligible age before 1984 probably is adding to the trend toward early retirement. One indication of the magnitude of the advantage is that the "replacement rate" is 20 percent higher for an average wage earner retiring in 1981 than for his counterpart who will retire after 1983, when the new benefit formula becomes mandatory. Moving the transition period forward by two years would save money for the system and also seems equitable because it would provide workers who retire in 1982 and 1983 the same benefits, relative to their wages just before retirement, as will be provided to subsequent retirees.

NOTES TO APPENDIX A

[1] As is discussed below, the new benefit formula becomes fully effective in 1984.

[2] Specifically, the alternative to the new formula benefit level is the level calculated under the old formula as of December 1978, adjusted upward for the subsequent increase in the CPI.

Appendix B

Short-Run Trust Fund Projections and Assumptions of the 1981 Trustees

---

TABLE B–1
Estimated Trust Fund Ratios for OASI, DI, and Medicare (HI) under 1981 Trustees' Five Projection Paths, Calendar Years 1980–1985

Fund/Projection Path[a]	1980[b]	1981	1982	1983	1984	1985
OASI						
Path I	23	18	14[c]	6[c]	—1[c]	—8[c]
Path II-A	23	18	13[c]	5[c]	—4[c]	—13[c]
Path II-B	23	18	13[c]	4[c]	[d]	[d]
Path III	23	18	13[c]	4[c]	[d]	[d]
"Worst-case"	23	18	13[c]	2[c]	[d]	[d]
DI						
Path I	35	20	13	35	66	104
Path II-A	35	20	13	33	62	96
Path II-B	35	20	13	32	58	87
Path III	35	20	13	31	52	75
"Worst-case"	35	20	13	29	47	68
OASDI						
Path I	25	18	14	9[c]	6[c]	4[c]
Path II-A	25	18	13	8[c]	3[c]	—1[c]
Path II-B	25	18	13	7[c]	2[c]	—5[c]
Path III	25	18	13	7[c]	[d]	[d]
"Worst-case"	25	18	13[c]	5[c]	[d]	[d]
HI						
Path I	52	46	58	69	77	82
Path II-A	52	46	57	66	70	70
Path II-B	52	46	57	64	67	65
Path III	52	46	56	62	60	53
"Worst-case"	52	46	56	61	60	55
OASDHI						
Path I	29	23	21	20	19	19
Path II-A	29	23	21	18	15	13

(Table continues)

TABLE B–1 (continued)

Fund/Projection Path[a]	1980[b]	1981	1982	1983	1984	1985
Path II-B	29	23	21	18	14	8[c]
Path III	29	23	21	17	9[c]	1[c]
"Worst-case"	29	23	20	15[c]	5[c]	[d]

[a] The economic assumptions underlying these projections paths are described in table B-2.

[b] Figures for 1980 represent actual experience.

[c] Assets of funds would be insufficient to pay benefits when due during part or all of this year.

[d] Assets are projected to be negative and are not projected to recover before the end of the long-range projection period.

SOURCE: Board of Trustees, Federal Old-Age and Survivors Insurance, Disability Insurance, and Hospital Insurance Trust Funds, *1981 Annual Report*, 1981, pp. 41, 114–15.

TABLE B–2

SELECTED ECONOMIC ASSUMPTIONS UNDERLYING 1981 TRUSTEES' FIVE PROJECTION PATHS, CALENDAR YEARS 1980–1985

Economic Assumption/ Projection Path	1980	1981	1982	1983	1984	1985
Real GNP						
(annual percent change)						
Path I	—0.1	1.7	4.8	5.3	4.7	4.4
Path II-A	—0.1	1.1	4.2	5.0	4.5	4.2
Path II-B	—0.1	1.1	3.7	3.5	2.9	2.9
Path III	—0.1	0.7	1.1	2.2	3.9	3.0
"Worst-Case"	—0.1	—0.1	0.7	0.7	4.4	4.4
CPI						
(annual percent change)						
Path I	13.5	10.7	8.3	6.5	5.0	4.1
Path II-A	13.5	11.1	8.3	6.2	5.5	4.7
Path II-B	13.5	11.1	9.4	9.0	8.2	7.4
Path III	13.5	12.6	12.5	11.1	10.7	9.7
"Worst-Case"	13.5	12.8	13.6	11.6	10.9	9.7
Average wages in						
covered employment						
(annual percent change)						
Path I	8.5	10.6	9.6	9.1	7.6	6.8
Path II-A	8.5	10.2	9.8	8.6	7.9	7.1
Path II-B	8.5	10.2	9.6	9.7	8.8	8.1
Path III	8.5	11.5	10.9	11.1	11.4	10.1
"Worst-Case"	8.5	10.6	11.0	10.3	12.0	10.4

TABLE B–2 (continued)

Economic Assumption/ Projection Path	1980	1981	1982	1983	1984	1985
Real wage differential (percentage points)[a]						
Path I	—5.0	—0.1	1.3	2.6	2.6	2.7
Path II-A	—5.0	—0.9	1.5	2.4	2.4	2.4
Path II-B	—5.0	—0.9	0.2	0.7	0.6	0.7
Path III	—5.0	—1.1	—1.6	0.0	0.7	0.4
"Worst-Case"	—5.0	—2.2	—2.6	—1.3	1.1	0.7
Unemployment rate (percent)						
Path I	7.1	7.7	7.1	6.5	6.0	5.7
Path II-A	7.1	7.8	7.2	6.6	6.4	5.9
Path II-B	7.1	7.8	7.5	7.2	7.0	6.8
Path III	7.1	7.9	8.0	8.8	7.9	7.4
"Worst-Case"	7.1	8.3	8.7	9.7	9.1	8.0

[a] The difference between the percentage increase in average annual wages in covered employment and the percentage increase in the average annual CPI.

SOURCE: *1981 Annual Report*, p. 29.

Appendix C

Summary of Recent Social Security Financing Reform Proposals

This appendix summarizes the social security financing proposals of the Reagan administration, Congressman J. J. Pickle in H.R. 3207, the NCSS, the President's Commission on Pension Policy, and the 1979 Advisory Council.

TABLE C-1
Summary of Recent Social Security Financing Reform Proposals

Proposal	Reagan Adminis-tration	H.R. 3207	NCSS	President's Commission on Pension Policy	1979 Advisory Council
Phase out student benefits	Yes	Yes	No	[a]	No
Phase out survivor benefits for parents of children aged 16 and 17	No	Yes	No	[a]	No
Eliminate minimum benefits and eliminate "windfall benefits"	[b]	[b]	[b]	Yes	[b]
Eliminate lump-sum death benefits	[c]	No	No	No	No
Phase out the retirement test	Yes	Yes	No	Yes	No
Tax a portion of social security benefits	No	No	No	[d]	[e]
Change the indexation of benefits	[f]	No	[g]	No	No
Extend coverage to all new government employees	No	No	Yes	Yes	Yes
Phase in increase in retirement age to 68	No	Yes	Yes	Yes	[h]
Change calculation of PIA and benefit adjustment factor	[i]	No	[j]	No	[k]
Alter current financing procedure	l	l,m	l,n	l,o	l,p

NOTES: A "yes" indicates support of a proposal or one similar in intent; a footnote letter indicates support with qualification; and a "no" indicates that the issue was either opposed or not addressed. Congressman J. J. Pickle is the author of H.R. 3207.

a The President's Commission on Pension Policy recommends that this provision be reexamined "and put on a more rational basis."

b The primary impact of the minimum benefit level and the "windfall benefits" received by persons with pensions from noncovered employment would be eliminated by complementing the elimination of the minimum benefits with either a pension offset procedure or by including an individual's noncovered earnings in the calculation of his or her AIME.

c The Reagan administration would eliminate lump-sum death benefits when there are no surviving family members.

d The President's Commission on Pension Policy would allow all payroll taxes to be deductible and would tax all benefits when received.

e The 1979 Advisory Council would tax one-half of benefits.

f The Reagan administration would delay from July 1982 to October 1982 the automatic benefit increase; thereafter, it would change the averaging period but would continue to index benefits to the CPI.

g The NCSS would index benefits by the lower of the percentage increase in wages or prices, but any declines in real benefits would be recaptured in years when real wages rise.

h The 1979 Advisory Council recommends that "serious consideration" be given to increasing the retirement age to sixty-eight.

i The Reagan administration would increase the benefit formula bend points by one-half (instead of 100 percent) of the increase in average covered wages from 1982 to 1987 and would reduce the benefits for early retirees so that a person retiring at age sixty-two would receive 55 percent of the PIA rather than the 80 percent provided under current law.

j The NCSS would change the benefit adjustment factors by increasing benefits for those who retire after sixty-five.

k The 1979 Advisory Council recommends a new benefit formula that would increase benefits for long-term, low-wage workers and for high-wage workers. The new benefit structure would have two brackets: 61 percent of the first $442 of AIME, plus 27 percent of AIME above $442.

l Interfund borrowing would be allowed. The Reagan administration proposal only implies that interfund borrowing would be allowed.

m H.R. 3207 would reallocate one-half of HI payroll taxes to the OASDI programs, reallocate a portion of DI taxes to OASI, and provide partial general fund financing of HI to compensate for the interfund reallocation.

n The NCSS would reduce (1) reduce the HI payroll tax rate by one-half and finance the remainder of HI from general revenues, (2) inject OASDI with one-half of the scheduled HI payroll taxes, and (3) cap OASDHI payroll tax rates at 18 percent and provide additional funds as needed from the general fund.

o The President's Commission on Pension Policy recommends an acceleration of the scheduled payroll tax rate increases.

p The 1979 Advisory Council recommends financing HI entirely through earmarked portions of the personal and corporate income taxes and diverting a portion of the HI payroll taxes to OASDI as needed to guarantee financial soundness. It also recommends borrowing from the Treasury and general fund financing during periods of high unemployment. It would effectively allow interfund borrowing by merging the trust funds.